Aligning School Districts as PLCs

Mark Van Clay
Perry Soldwedel
Thomas W. Many

Solution Tree | Press

a division of
Solution Tree

555 North Morton Street
Bloomington, IN 47404
800.733.6786 (toll free) / 812.336.7700
FAX: 812.336.7790

email: info@solution-tree.com
solution-tree.com

Printed in the United States of America

15 14 13 12 11   1 2 3 4 5

FSC
Mixed Sources
Product group from well-managed
forests and other controlled sources

Cert no. SW-COC-002283
www.fsc.org
© 1996 Forest Stewardship Council

Library of Congress Cataloging-in-Publication Data

Van Clay, Mark.
  Aligning school districts as PLCs / Mark Van Clay, Perry Soldwedel, Thomas W. Many.
      p. cm.
  Includes bibliographical references and index.
  ISBN 978-1-935543-39-8 (perfect bound) -- ISBN 978-1-935543-40-4 (library edition)
  1. School districts--United States. 2. Professional learning communities--United States. I. Soldwedel, Perry. II. Many, Thomas W. III. Title.
  LB2817.3V36 2011
  379.1'535--dc22
                              2011006148

Solution Tree
Jeffrey C. Jones, CEO & President

Solution Tree Press
President: Douglas M. Rife
Publisher: Robert D. Clouse
Vice President of Production: Gretchen Knapp
Managing Production Editor: Caroline Wise
Senior Production Editor: Edward M. Levy
Copy Editor: Rachel Rosolina
Proofreader: David Eisnitz
Text Designer: Amy Shock
Cover Designer: Orlando Angel

To Karen, my life's compass to true north. You have shown me the best of what alignment between two people can be. —Mark Van Clay

To Rita, whose love, encouragement, and support inspires me to continue my career passion, and to my grandchildren—Tyler, Finley, Avery, and Hazel—who I hope will benefit from greater educational system accountability. —Perry Soldwedel

To Susan, who taught me that a life well lived means to "give without remembering and receive without forgetting." Without her loving support and encouragement, my part of this project would not have been written. —Thomas W. Many

Acknowledgments

Perry and Mark are grateful for their experiences with the Consortium for Educational Change (CEC), an Illinois-based group that is invested in collaborative leadership models and continuous improvement work with school districts. Through CEC, both have had numerous opportunities to put concepts from this book into practice in real school districts during real time. As a result, this effort represents far more than theory, because what is described here has been successfully applied.

Tom is grateful to the faculty and staff of Kildeer Countryside Community Consolidated School District 96, who have worked tirelessly to faithfully implement the tenets of the professional learning communities model in their schools. It is only through their unwavering commitment to ensuring that *all* children reach their maximum potential that District 96 has become one of the premier elementary school districts in the nation.

* * *

Solution Tree Press would like to thank the following reviewers:

Jeffrey K. Butts
Assistant Superintendent
Metropolitan School District of Wayne
  Township
Indianapolis, Indiana

Anne Conzemius
Co-Founder and President
QLD Learning
Madison, Wisconsin

Debra Dees
Principal
Brookwood High School
Snellville, Georgia

Patrick Duncan
Associate Superintendent of Schools
Greater Victoria School District (No. 61)
Victoria, British Columbia

Richard Goodman
Consultant
New England School Development
  Council
Hampton, New Hampshire

Robin Hall
Executive Director, Regional System of
  District & School Support, Region 4
Alameda County, California

Dennis King
Assistant Superintendent of School
   Improvement
Blue Valley School District
Overland Park, Kansas

Carrie VanAlstine
Assistant Superintendent of Curriculum
   and Instruction
Ball-Chatham Community Unit School
District #5
Chatham, Illinois

Visit **go.solution-tree.com/plcbooks** to download the
reproducibles in this book.

Table of Contents

About the Authors

Mark Van Clay is a consultant specializing in boards of education, strategic visioning, and system assessments for schools and districts. He also consults through the Consortium for Educational Change (CEC), an Illinois-based network of school districts specializing in continuous organizational improvement. Mark is coauthor of *The School Board Fieldbook: Leading With Vision* (2009) and has published multiple articles in state and national professional journals.

Mark has consulted in the areas of collaborative leadership, performance scorecards and dashboards, systems and role alignment, strategic visioning, continuous improvement models and strategies, reporting through data, shared revenue models in collective bargaining contracts, student management as a behavior curriculum, and the application of instructional theory to classroom practice.

A twenty-two-year superintendent whose leadership experiences include wealthy, financially challenged, and ethnically diverse school districts, Mark is also a former principal, elementary teacher, and instructor in gifted writing for schools in suburban Chicago.

As a superintendent and principal, Mark's leadership led to U.S. Department of Education Blue Ribbon School Awards for two schools, one in a wealthy suburban district and the other in an ethnically diverse school. Mark holds degrees from Northern Illinois University, Purdue University Calumet, and DePauw University.

Perry Soldwedel is the director of continuous improvement for the Consortium of Educational Change. CEC is a not-for-profit consortium of some eighty Illinois school districts that work together to accelerate behaviors and actions leading to organizational growth and improvement. His expertise is in the areas of shared leadership, system assessment, strategic visioning, data collection and measurement, information/analysis, accountability, and the alignment of standards, assessments, and instruction.

Perry is a former school district superintendent, assistant superintendent for curriculum and instruction, technology director, principal, assistant principal, and elementary and middle school teacher, all in the state of Illinois. His district received two Blue Ribbon School awards and was the recipient of a $3.5 million U.S. Department of Education Technology Challenge Grant. The district also received a Lincoln/Baldrige award. He has taught continuing education classes for the University of Illinois. He is coauthor of *The School Board Fieldbook: Leading With Vision* (2009).

Perry received his three degrees from the University of Illinois, Bradley University, and Western Illinois University.

Thomas W. Many, former superintendent of Kildeer Countryside Community Consolidated School District 96 in Buffalo Grove, Illinois, keeps a sharp focus on school improvement issues. He uses the tenets of professional learning communities (PLC) to ensure that all students are able to reach their maximum potential.

Student achievement in District 96 has improved every year for twelve consecutive years. More than 95 percent of all students now meet or exceed state standards. The district has been especially effective in helping students with special needs improve their academic performance. Under Tom's leadership, District 96 has become recognized as one of the premier elementary school districts in the nation.

Tom's long and distinguished career includes twenty years of experience as a superintendent. He has also served as a classroom teacher, learning center director, curriculum supervisor, principal, and assistant superintendent. A dedicated PLC practitioner, Tom is a compelling and sought-after speaker and coauthor of *Learning by Doing: A Handbook for Professional Learning Communities at Work* (2006, 2010) with Rick DuFour, Rebecca DuFour, and Robert Eaker.

To book Mark Van Clay, Perry Soldwedel, or Thomas W. Many for professional development, contact pd@solution-tree.com.

Foreword

By Michael Fullan

When professional learning communities (PLCs) first became popular, there were two problems. One was that the term was used superficially, with the result that PLCs became hard to define in practice. The other was that they were confined to single schools. Thanks to the DuFours and their colleagues, we have moved forward on both fronts. The three big ideas began to anchor PLCs: ensuring that all students can learn, building a collaborative culture, and establishing a focus on results. PLCs have become a districtwide phenomenon. The culture of the whole district has now become the focus.

Aligning School Districts as PLCs takes us deeply into districtwide reform. Its three authors have been steeped in the doing of change, but they have also been reflective practitioners. Hence, their insights are specific and thorough. Unlike others who have written on district reform, Van Clay, Soldwedel, and Many show us both sides of how to implement PLCs: they illustrate clearly and painfully what can go wrong, but equally clearly, they tell us how easily these problems can be avoided or addressed.

First, they offer a strong framework—not only the three big ideas, but also a process framework consisting of strategic, tactical, and operational dimensions. This three-part frame is used throughout the book, and for the careful reader will become a new habit and a guide to systemic thinking about all aspects of districtwide PLC reform. It represents just enough theory to cover all key components of policy and implementation, and just the right amount of practical insight to sort out what should be done, and what could go wrong.

What is particularly brilliant about the book is that in each chapter they present a grounded, hypothetical case of a composite district called "Nirvana," and trace how its leaders go about introducing PLCs. The entire cast is represented: school board members, parents and community, the superintendent and other district leaders, principals, teachers, and students. One sees things go wrong despite the fact that certain issues are attended to well, because others are neglected. You see a superintendent do a superb job of selling the board on collaboration yet fail to do the same for schools. You see the development of a data assessment system that, while sophisticated, ends up being detached from its larger purpose, and from daily usability.

Once the authors present and apply their framework, it is easy to see the solutions. I love the way they dissect what occurred at Nirvana—first by describing what was done right, and then by showing what was done wrong. By the time they have taken us through this process a few times, we begin to understand more deeply and more practically how PLCs should be introduced.

Two things especially stick with me. One is that we see just how easy it is to go wrong with a great idea. But then we also come to see how easy it is to go "right." While it is easy to make mistakes along the way, it is not all that difficult to implement PLCs once you know what you are doing. This is always the beauty of informed practitioners. They make powerful reform more understandable and more doable.

I was struck by the similarities between district and system change. I have borrowed the term *simplexity* to capture this strategic knowledge (Fullan, 2010). The simple part is that there are a small number of key components that you need to attend to. These are not difficult to grasp, and they are small enough in number so as not to be overwhelming. The complex part concerns how to make these components jell in combination: we must deal with the social complexity of working with groups, the political complexity of linking different levels and interests, and the logistical complexity of having to make decisions in highly charged and rapidly moving change processes.

The ideas in this book will stick with you. You will remember the mistakes made in Nirvana, understand clearly how they could have been made, and realize (in retrospect) how obviously consequential they were. But more deeply, you will see the decisions and actions that should have been taken. You will be much smarter about districtwide reform after reading this book.

Michael Fullan is professor emeritus at the Ontario Institute for Studies in Education of the University of Toronto.

Fullan, M. (2010) *Motion leadership: The skinny on becoming change savvy.* Thousand Oaks, CA: Corwin Press.

Introduction

This book is about how a school district can purposefully align its efforts toward becoming a professional learning community (PLC). In particular, it examines how districts can align themselves to the three big ideas of PLCs: (1) ensuring a focus on learning, (2) building a collaborative culture, and (3) establishing a results orientation.

Professional learning communities have profoundly changed how teachers and principals approach the work of schooling. Yet many districts fail to consistently support PLC efforts. While PLCs have clearly identified the classroom essentials necessary for continually improved student learning, districts have not always created the supportive structures to make that happen, even when being a PLC is their intent.

The result? It is much harder to establish and sustain a districtwide PLC than it needs to be. The missing ingredient is an understanding of alignment and how it affects all efforts within a district.

We arrived at this conclusion by combining our own experiences with the insights of six renowned educators to whom we are deeply indebted. Richard DuFour, Rebecca DuFour, and Robert Eaker (2008) have spent more than a decade eloquently defining and developing professional learning communities. In particular, they have made a compelling case for looking at classroom teachers as part of grade-level or department teams, rather than as independent contractors working in isolation. Their book *Revisiting Professional Learning Communities at Work*™ seeks to show how school and district work should similarly extend from the work of PLC teams.

We also draw on the work of Michael Fullan, who has spent much of the last decade writing about "capacity building" (2005), defined as the effort of districts (as well as regional, state, and federal agencies) to support classroom efforts to continuously improve student learning. Fullan has spoken eloquently about the powerful impact that aligning policies, practices, and procedures across multiple systems has on success. Here we focus on how to align policies, practices, and procedures across a district to maximize results.

Finally, Robert Marzano and Tim Waters (2009) have provided insights into three related areas: (1) the importance of identifying certain key concepts as districtwide "givens" or non-negotiables, (2) the positive impact of effective school and district-level leadership on student achievement, and (3) the need for aligning board of education actions to provide required district resources. We borrow from their insights in our descriptions of alignment districtwide.

To this powerful body of educational theory and research we add two additional concepts from our own experiences. First, we define three distinct organizational roles found within every district—the strategic, the tactical, and the operational—and explore how these roles interact with the notion of alignment. Second, we identify a variety of data-based reporting strategies in an attempt to demonstrate the importance of aligning data across all district levels.

We therefore borrow from many elements of theory, research, and practice to present a practical approach to successfully aligning professional learning communities, from the classroom to the board of education. The key to this approach is in recognizing the power of districtwide alignment.

As a metaphor for alignment, think of a compass. Just as the compass, which points to true north, helps travelers stay on course during long journeys over vast distances, so aligning the activities of everyone in a district toward the big ideas of a PLC helps districts stay on course toward the common goal of high levels of learning for all.

We three joined forces for this book to extol the virtues of alignment as applied to professional learning communities. It represents the perfect nexus between Perry and Mark's systems orientations and Tom's professional learning communities expertise and experiences. It also represents an opportunity for Tom and Mark to team once again—something they have been waiting to do since their doctoral work together many years ago. We found our own alignment through our collaboration and benefited from each other's perspectives as lifelong educators with differing but complementary skills. Each of us learned from this experience as much as we gave.

It is our intention to provide leaders at all levels of a district with an instrument that is both theoretically sound and practically useful. To that end, *Aligning School Districts as PLCs* offers accessible and easily replicable observations and examples.

Chapter 1 establishes the notion of alignment by using brief "sound bites" from the perspectives of the three district roles. These examples illustrate the difficulty of aligning a district's policies, practices, and procedures at all levels, even when there are shared beliefs that supposedly link them in common cause. Chapter 1 also introduces the three "big ideas" of PLCs. If alignment is seen as a guiding compass, then the three big ideas represent the destination that compass is leading them toward.

Chapter 2 focuses on four essentials needed for district alignment: (1) district roles, (2) communication through data, (3) loose and tight leadership, and (4) what we refer to as *alignment constants*—non-negotiable actions that are the same across all of the big ideas. These four alignment constants must be in place in order for a district's alignment efforts to be successful. Applications of each of them are presented and discussed.

Chapters 3, 4, and 5 show aligned PLC practices. This is accomplished by identifying role-based responsibilities that address the non-negotiables for each of the big ideas. We also look at how the alignment constants apply to each big idea. Finally, we tell a story in each of these chapters that illustrates a *lack* of alignment and the changes an aligned approach would make to that story. Each of these three chapters focuses on one of the big ideas.

Chapter 6 presents two tools to help a district answer the questions, How are we doing in successfully aligning ourselves? How can we objectively tell?

The appendix (page 135) contains reproducible big idea appraisal tools (also found online at **go.solution-tree.com/plcbooks**) that schools can use to determine how far along they are with respect to implementation. Readers may want to consult these tools as they work through the book.

The positive impact of professional learning communities on children and teachers and in classrooms is irrefutable. But how much greater an impact might PLCs demonstrate if we could change not just one classroom, department, or team at a time, but an entire district at a time! We believe attention to alignment at a districtwide level can significantly contribute to that outcome.

Mark Van Clay

Perry Soldwedel

Thomas Many

chapter one

The Case for Districtwide Alignment

> He who loves practice without theory is like a sailor who boards a ship without a rudder and a compass and never knows where he may cast.
>
> —Leonardo da Vinci

The notion of alignment assumes a coordinated effort that results in successfully melding various parts of a system. When these parts are aligned, the outcomes are more predictable, more efficiently attained, and more likely to be the result that was desired.

Some districts, however, are like a highly trained athlete who suffers an injury. If the athlete continues to perform by trying to compensate for the injury, other injuries inevitably develop in other parts of his body. A pitcher who injures a knee will often develop a sore shoulder or elbow.

In a similar fashion, efforts break down when different levels within the district are not functioning in mutually supportive and connected ways. Since each level is tethered to the other levels, a problem in one affects all of them.

Clearly, those who teach the children represent the most critical level around which to align. But those who don't teach still need to provide the resources, vision, foci, learning environment, accountability structures, and common messages required to support those who do.

How can all parts interrelate and interconnect in ways that allow a district to best deliver its full potential as a professional learning community?

We define *districtwide alignment* as *the intentional linkage of the work of schools and the school district to the work of collaborative teams in order to achieve a districtwide professional learning community.*

For public schools, alignment is the bridge between theory and practice; alignment is about how to successfully approach the challenge of having *all* levels of the district support what will actually work with real children in real classroom settings.

It's Not Easy

This alignment business is not easy to do. School districts are multilayered structures in which many roles and responsibilities operate simultaneously. Students, classroom teachers, support teachers, teacher aides, nonteaching staff, department heads, school administrators, district administrators, union leaders, and boards of education each make their own contributions—not to mention influences outside of the district such as parents, community interests, politicians, policymakers, state and federal education bodies, educational publishers, and university schools of education.

Yet the thought of all of these moving parts acting in ballet-like coordination seems daunting when considering how complex the interactions among the different levels of a district can become. Let's explore these interactions by looking at the fictional Nirvana School District. Here, a message to set rigorous, districtwide achievement targets for students is interpreted differently by the school board, the superintendent, the high school principal, and the teachers association president.

The School Board's Perspective———————————

The board's new goals were tied to two rigorous student achievement targets that computer programmer and board member George Bell had crafted. These targets were: (1) to be at the top of the list of in-state student achievement scores for demographically similar schools and (2) to be at the 75th percentile compared to a list of high-achieving exemplar schools. The two comparisons would be made for each Nirvana school, followed by a ranking of all the Nirvana schools in terms of how they compared to each other.

It was the board's intent to devote a full meeting to this presentation, so the public could be well informed. Board president Fran Ackers thought, with satisfaction, that these outcome measures would define the district's progress and increase academic rigor. And since they had started with some easy practice targets last year to get everyone used to the idea, real targets, she reasoned, shouldn't be scary to anyone now.

The board, as you can see, is justifiably proud of its efforts to set more rigorous student achievement goals and targets. It is committed to improving the achievement of its students and has taken initiative to do so. Since the staff had used practice targets that were not publicized last year, the board believed its newest action represented the first tangible step in seriously addressing academic rigor.

Let's see if the superintendent agrees.

The Superintendent's Perspective

Superintendent Sue Stanfield thought the targets themselves certainly gave clear direction around expected improvement, but she knew that the underlying preparatory steps needed to reach them in classrooms were not in place.

For one thing, last year's practice targets showed just how much there was to learn about how to effectively use data. Sue knew there would still need to be a considerable amount of staff training in how to collect, manage, and properly interpret data at classroom and building levels. Moreover, the administration and teachers had not had any input into the districtwide targets that were set. She saw real trouble there!

Beyond that significant issue, there would also have to be a change in scheduling so department teams could meet on a regular basis to work with the data they would be generating. And changing schedules would be a major issue to resolve with the Nirvana Teachers Union—never a speedy process. Sue was worried. There were a lot of things to implement, even before they could hope to concentrate fully on the board's targets. "How are we going to be able to ratchet things up so quickly?" she wondered. "And how can I get the board to pull back for a while yet still understand I am supportive of its goal of increased academic rigor?"

Clearly, the superintendent is not facing these new student achievement targets with nearly the same enthusiasm level as the board. It isn't that she doesn't favor more academic rigor—she does—but at the moment, she is concerned with how to address all of the necessary underlying staff preparation when there doesn't seem to be time to do so. Moreover, Sue strongly suspects her administrators and teachers will not respond well to achievement targets they had no say in setting. As a result, she is anticipating that significant political and logistical issues will dominate the rest of this school year for her, just when her full attention should be on helping the principals meet their targets.

Are her good intentions being acknowledged at the school level?

The Teachers Association's Perspective

Teachers association president Barbara King had an intense conversation with Phil Modine, a principal in the district. The new board goals and their data-based targets are completely unfair, Barbara had told him in no uncertain terms. It seemed to her that the only possible reason for the board to put such exacting targets in place was to publicly embarrass the Nirvana teachers. Why else would they publicly announce such lofty targets?

For Barbara, it was telling that the teachers association was neither consulted nor involved in identifying and establishing the targets. Didn't the board realize how scary it had been for teachers to even agree to set practice targets last year? And why wasn't the board celebrating the fact that every Nirvana school except one had either met or surpassed those targets?

Barbara felt that she had just been handed a "gotcha." No one had recognized all of the teachers' hard work in achieving the practice targets, and now there were newer, tougher targets as their "reward" for cooperating in good faith. She felt betrayed and was plenty angry about it!

The principal, as you will see, obviously has anything but enthusiasm for the new board targets.

The Principal's Perspective

Phil didn't always see eye to eye with Barbara, but he was mostly in agreement this time. He was particularly concerned about the within-district target comparisons. His school was not the wealthy Nirvana high school on the east side of town. His was the one on the other side of the tracks, with a 38 percent mobility rate, and half of his students were on free or reduced lunches. He knew it was just a matter of time before he would be publicly berated by the board for his scores.

What was the matter with Sue Stanfield that she would let the board do something like this? What was the district office doing up there? It was clear to Phil he was facing some big problems, and he would very likely be facing them on his own.

He sees trouble on every side: the teachers will blame him for unfair target comparisons, no input, and inadequate training; he can't depend on the superintendent or the district office to be of any help; and the board's targets will surely make him—and his school—look bad by comparison. Since the district office let this happen, they are either powerless before the board or in league with it. Either way, it's now evident he will get no help from them. Meeting the targets is the least of the principal's concerns right now. He has plenty of his own issues to contend with.

Given four such differing perspectives on the supposedly common effort of increasing academic rigor, there is little promise of success. This effort appears doomed from the start.

On the other hand, what if the board, the superintendent, the association president, and the principal were all aligned in their efforts? Surely none of them are *against* increasing academic rigor. What if there were common agreement on what targets the goals should reach? On what types of staff training would be required? On how much training would be provided before results were publicly reported? And on which types of data would be reported, and to whom? How might this story have turned out differently if answers to these questions had been collaboratively determined early in the game, rather than becoming areas of contention after the initiative was already under way?

This is a small example of the kind of missed opportunities for alignment that occur every day in most districts. It shows why alignment is hard work and why it cannot be addressed intuitively or serendipitously. Although a deeper level of coordination could have made this Nirvana effort far more likely to succeed, such coordination does not come without a lot of careful thought, collaborative planning, and focused communication.

The Three Big Ideas

If alignment is the compass by which school leaders guide the school district's journey to becoming a professional learning community, then the destination is best represented by the three big ideas of a PLC. DuFour, et al. (2008) define these ideas as (1) ensuring that all students learn, (2) building a collaborative culture, and (3) establishing a focus on results.

Ensuring That All Students Learn

Ensuring that all students learn requires a focus on learning instead of teaching. The emphasis is on what children know and what they next need to learn.

Madeline Hunter (1976) understands the value of sound teaching and its relationship to learning, but she emphasizes the act of teaching as a direct causal agent for learning, rather than the learning itself: "When teachers' plans are based on valid content and sound theory, then implemented with artistry that incorporates fundamental values of human learning, *students will learn*. When those principles of human learning are violated or neglected, learning will be impeded" (p. 1). DuFour et al. (2008) took Hunter's observation one step further: the first big idea doesn't negate or discount sound instruction; rather, it views teaching as a means to an end rather than an end in itself.

Building a Collaborative Culture

DuFour et al. (2008) also stress the innate commonalities of a learning community: "Community suggests a group linked by common interests. Communities form around common characteristics, experiences, practices, or beliefs that are important enough to bind its members to one another in a meaningful collaboration" (pp. 19–20).

Michael Fullan and Andy Hargreaves (1996, p. x, italics added) define *community* in similar terms when they state that "collegiality and individuality are not incompatible. They can and must go together if we are to improve our schools. Our message is about working *together* for improvement."

This second big idea acknowledges that it is far likelier students will learn if they are taught by adults who are always learning themselves, especially when the adults are learning about how students learn. This requires that teachers become their own learning communities and that, as Fullan and Hargreaves and DuFour, DuFour, and Eaker point out, their learning be collaborative rather than isolated, grounded in research and best practices, and informed by sound formative and summative assessment data.

Establishing a Focus on Results

The third big idea means that results need to drive decisions and subsequent actions. Kaplan and Miyake (2010) note that "the simple act of measuring and monitoring causes people to pay attention to what is measured" (p. 11).

This is a significant commitment, because there are all sorts of activities around the fringes of student learning—teacher competencies and skills, efficiencies in expenditures per student, the adoptions of the latest and most widely praised curricula—that can be taken as results to make a school or a district look good, even when the student learning itself does not change.

The challenge is to obtain results that reflect what is actually learned in classrooms. This puts a premium on precisely matching results to learning expectations and using those results to track progress. Even the most credible measures of student learning improve, flatline, or recede, but for a successful PLC journey, only one of those results can suffice.

Conclusion

Given the differing perspectives that are natural in a typical district, aligning district-wide efforts is not easy to do. Yet alignment is nevertheless the most hospitable environment for a PLC. The focus for alignment should be the three big ideas: ensuring that all students learn, building a collaborative culture, and establishing a focus on results. These three ideas make the goal of functioning as a PLC tangible at each district level.

The next chapter looks more deeply into the nature of alignment. What are the essential elements that alignment requires, and how do they work?

chapter two

Alignment's Essential Components

It can really be off-putting when you lose your way somehow.
—Winnie-the-Pooh

This chapter will discuss how alignment works by highlighting its four essential elements: (1) defining district roles, (2) communicating through data, (3) applying loose and tight leadership, and (4) applying the alignment constants. Just as the component parts of a compass need to be working well in order to determine your course, these essential elements of alignment must all be in good working order for efforts at alignment to be effective.

Defining District Roles

In looking at district roles, we first examine the types of roles, then the phenomenon of role bridges, and finally the cascading effect that roles have on each other.

The Three Roles

There are three distinct district roles—strategic, tactical, and operational—in every district (Van Clay & Soldwedel, 2009). Who assumes each role, how well they assume it, and how their actions affect those in other roles determine how successfully a school district will reach its desired state of alignment.

The Strategic Role

The strategic role is responsible for articulating big-picture, visionary views of what the district wants to accomplish over the long term. It is customer-focused, responsible for establishing the mission, vision, values, and overarching strategic goals, and committed to monitoring, through data, the results of the district's efforts around those strategic goals.

In a typical district, strategists are boards of education, often in partnership with the superintendent. In a well-aligned district, that partnership also includes union leadership. The board sets strategic direction by issuing charges to the administration to create plans by which to carry out and monitor the strategic goals. To use a home construction analogy, the strategic responsibility identifies the criteria, including all the applicable codes, for designing the house. It does not create the blueprints (tactical) or build the house (operational).

The Tactical Role

The tactical role is responsible for crafting and carrying out the plans that address the strategic goals. The tactical role is organization-focused—it is responsible for planning how to meet the mission, vision, values, and strategic goals. It allocates the resources to meet those goals and sets up monitoring systems by which to measure progress.

Tacticians are typically district administrators and principals. District administrators have districtwide tactical responsibilities, while principals have building-level tactical responsibilities. In a well-aligned district, tactical responsibilities are shared with department chairs and team leaders. The successful implementation of a PLC requires that district and building planning efforts align.

The Operational Role

The operational role implements tactical plans. Operationalists must "field test" tactical plans to see if they work in real time with real children in real classrooms. Tactical plans that do not field test well have to be revised before they can be effectively implemented.

The operational role is student-focused and is responsible for meeting strategic goals through a direct impact on student learning. Operationalists are primarily teachers, but may include other staff members, such as instructional coaches, curricular specialists, or paraprofessionals, who may not teach children directly but are immersed in instructional and curricular work at the classroom level.

Role Bridges

Because each role has its own area of expertise, each views events through its own perspective. This means each role can have the same experience but see, feel, and interpret that experience very differently.

The Nirvana vignette in chapter 1 (pp. 6–8) illustrates just how differently the three roles can view the same experiences. From its strategic perspective, the board viewed targets as an exciting first step in establishing more academic rigor in the district. However, the superintendent had tactical concerns that too many things were not in place for to the board's vision to be successfully implemented. The principal, also with a tactical perspective, was concerned about the controversy the targets had created in his school and the way he and the school were publicly perceived. At the operational level, the teachers' union president felt the targets were a public slap at the district's teachers.

Thus, actions taken by an enthusiastic board were met with unanticipated and unproductive reactions from the superintendent (who was worried), the union president (who was angry), and the principal (who felt abandoned). Even under the best conditions, it can be difficult for roles to communicate accurately with each other. Fortunately, however, a typical district has certain positions that lend themselves to serving as bridges between roles.

At their most effective, superintendents are bridges between the strategic and tactical roles, operating equally well in both, and principals naturally bridge between the tactical and operational roles.

Effective superintendents are natural bridges, because they usually possess equally high levels of strategic and tactical knowledge, understanding, and skill. An effective superintendent can both conceptualize long-range visions and goals and actualize them through planning and resource distribution decisions. This makes the superintendent's position well suited to accurately communicate the board's strategic message, while helping shape the tactical responses of the district office administrators.

Although most no longer teach, effective principals possess a keen ear for the perspectives and needs of teachers. They can usually align reasonable tactical requirements from the district office to the needs and aspirations of their teaching staff.

Teacher leaders can also be effective bridges. Because teacher leaders, such as union presidents or other officers, have responsibilities for running their own organizations, they have the ability to communicate with administrators and board members through their own tactical and strategic understandings, even though they represent an operational perspective.

These bridge positions can be excellent sounding boards for assessing the state of overall communication in a district. When bridge positions function effectively, districtwide alignment efforts are enhanced. When they don't, there is widespread miscommunication, misrepresentation, and misinformation across roles.

For example, in the Nirvana story, had board, administrative, and teacher leaders been in regular communication, issues over the setting of targets, of what data should be reported to whom, and the amount and time frame for data training could all have been worked out before any implementation was announced by the board. These collaborative discussions across bridge roles could have enhanced implementation, because none of the tactical and operational concerns that were voiced required the abandonment of targets.

The Cascading Effect

The cascading effect illustrates how the strategic and tactical district roles can easily, even if unintentionally, generate more work for other roles. A single strategic decision will usually result in a few tactical tasks that will, in turn, result in multiple operational responsibilities.

The cascading effect is visually illustrated in table 2.1. Here, a single strategic decision for one non-negotiable results in two tactical responsibilities and seven operational responsibilities. This phenomenon represents the natural progression of work across roles. When moving from more general (strategic) to more specific (operational) work, it is logical to expect that "more specific" inevitably leads to "more responsibilities."

A failure to recognize the operational impact of a strategic decision due to the cascading effect is a major reason strategists and tacticians frequently get "My plate is too full" feedback from teachers, regardless of the merits of the change being proposed. Strategists and tacticians in turn become more entrenched in their responses ("They always complain about being too busy") and begin making decisions that are more appropriately operational ("This is too important to wait, so we'll push it through despite all the complaining!").

How does an aligned district avoid such operational overload and strategic and tactical overreach while still pursuing needed changes?

First, strategists should stick to a few strategic goals and stay with them for several years. It is easier for those at the tactical and operational levels to refine and improve a goal from a previous year than it is to continually start over with a new one.

Second, any overload of the district's capacity for change becomes the responsibility of tacticians, who best understand the capacity of the district as a whole but don't feel the stress of being overloaded with strategic initiatives as keenly as do teachers.

The cascading effect doesn't have to prove fatal to implementing change, but it does have to be accounted for. Otherwise, a district risks having its initiatives drowned by issues that don't contribute to the successful implementation of a PLC.

Communicating Through Data

We support the notion of utilizing data, converted to information, as evidence of learning (DuFour et al., 2008). But we also see data as one of the four essential components of district alignment. As we discuss data later in this chapter, we will reference data's evidence role as well as its alignment potentials.

To illustrate, consider again the Nirvana vignette. The board was excited to set an aggressive achievement goal for the district, but that goal—attaining at the 75th percentile proficiency level—caused responses that ran from excitement to concern to insult. That different roles receive different messages from the same data should be no surprise, but data need to ease efforts toward districtwide alignment, not complicate them. To understand how data can work for or against alignment, we will first describe the characteristics of data as a communications tool and then look at the four ways it functions in alignment.

Table 2.1: The Cascading Effect

Strategic	Tactical	Operational
1. Approve school system curricular goals aligned to state standards and translated into common student learning targets expressed by class, course, or grade level.	1.1 Establish essential learning targets that represent what each student should learn as a result of a class, course, or grade level.	1.1.1 Develop essential learning targets that represent what each student should know and be able to do as a result of a class, course, or grade level.
		1.1.2 Translate essential learning targets into student-friendly language, and provide examples or models of the target.
		1.1.3 Deconstruct essential learning targets to identify prerequisite skills necessary to reach mastery.
		1.1.4 Engage in annual review and revision of essential learning targets.
	1.2 Develop and implement training programs and timelines for teachers to understand and use essential learning targets in their instruction.	1.2.1 Acquire the knowledge, skills, tools, and strategies to translate the goals to common essential learning targets in daily classroom practice.
		1.2.2 Use the knowledge, skills, tools, and strategies in common essential learning targets through unit and daily lesson plans.
		1.2.3 Use the knowledge, skills, tools, and strategies to evaluate the appropriateness of the common essential learning targets.
2. Require equitable access to the guaranteed and viable curriculum for all students.	2.1 Monitor implementation of the guaranteed and viable curriculum to ensure equitable access for all students.	2.1.1 Prioritize and consistently focus instruction on the essential learning targets for all students.
		2.1.2 Exercise professional discretion over how to teach the essential learning targets.
		2.1.3 Develop pacing guides to set the sequence and pacing of instruction.
		2.1.4 Design and deliver lessons that teach to the essential learning targets.

We define data characteristics based on the SMART goal work of Conzemius and O'Neill (2002), who tie data to measures that directly assess improved student learning. SMART goals are:

Strategic and **S**pecific

Measurable

Attainable

Results oriented

Time bound (p. 4)

Individual student learning goals are *strategically* linked to district learning goals and are *specific* to particular outcomes; *measurable*, so whether the learning goal was attained or not can be objectively assessed; *attainable*, so the learning goal is challenging, yet not out of reach for the student; *results oriented*, so what is being measured is reflective of something important to be learned; and *time bound*, so there is an expectation about when learning should be completed, in order that subsequent learning can follow in an orderly, sequenced fashion.

Table 2.2 shows an example of a district SMART goal. Note how measures align to indicators, which align to the goal. This alignment thread of goal to indicator to measure is the essence of a SMART goal.

Table 2.2: District Long-Range Strategic Plan SMART Goal

Goal: We will continuously improve student growth and achievement.	
Indicators	**Measures**
Students entering "kindergarten ready"	Kindergarten readiness assessment
Students meeting/exceeding expectations on state assessments comparable to benchmark districts	State test
Students meeting/exceeding district grade-level/course learning expectations	District benchmark/course assessments
Students meeting/exceeding personal goals	NWEA MAP growth assessments
Number of students in advanced placement courses at middle and high school increasing	Advanced placement enrollment
Performance gaps between subgroup populations decreasing	Subgroup performance assessment/state test/district benchmark/course assessment
Students make successful transition to middle and high school	First semester grades

SMART goals offer a structure by which data can more accurately and commonly be understood across differing roles, which in turn augments districtwide alignment efforts.

Alignment is served:

- Through collecting formative and summative assessment data
- By comparing data to analyze them for meaning and implications
- By presenting data in specific ways according to audience
- From reporting on data using appropriate reporting tools

Collecting Formative and Summative Assessments

Formative assessments inform teachers about which students are learning what and at what pace; summative assessments are designed to generate cumulative end-point determinations that answer the question, was the expected learning mastered or not?

Sam Redding (2006) suggests that formative assessments are best viewed as learning activities. Quick diagnostic tests—pencil-and-paper tests, oral quizzes, or "show-me" assessments—enable students to demonstrate their level of mastery and allow teachers to make instructional adjustments during the teaching and learning process. (What makes an assessment either formative or summative is how the results of the assessment are used—not the particular assessment itself.)

Formative assessments need to be frequent, since waiting weeks or months to assess how students are progressing through the curriculum is hardly a timely process. Short cycles of assessment provide teachers with regular feedback and allow teams to coordinate their intervention efforts. Formative assessments are also most powerful when they are common to all the members of a team who teach the same class, course, or grade level. This commonality allows teachers in the same departments or grades to measure the same things in the same ways.

If formative assessments are about generating ongoing diagnostic information that allows for timely and focused interventions, summative assessments enable teacher teams to see how students have progressed toward mastery of standards that will be included on state assessments. Summative assessments provide useful data to the system as a whole and are not given as frequently as formative assessments.

Redding (2006) points out that summative assessments provide a measure not only of student progress but of school progress by subject area and grade level, and that they are most useful in making programmatic and placement decisions.

Data Comparisons

This is the second of the four alignment applications of data. There are three kinds of data comparisons: (1) to results over time, (2) to similar groups, and (3) to high achievers or exemplars. As with formative and summative assessment data, none of these options alone gives as comprehensive a view of results as the combination of all of them.

The comparisons of *results over time* show trends over a number of years. An example would be comparing state reading scores from this year to the same school's state reading scores over the last five years.

Similar group comparisons of data show whether achievement is at, above, or below a general trend line. An example would be comparing the school's state reading scores to schools with similar demographic and financial characteristics.

Comparisons to exemplars show where one's achievement results are in relation to the very best. An example would be comparing the school's reading scores to those of top-performing schools, regardless of their demographic or financial situation. The comparative question here is simple: what does the very best in achievement look like compared to what we are doing?

This three-level system of comparisons guarantees that there will always be "stretch" targets for continuous improvement. Even when comparisons against one's own previous results are improving, there are still comparisons to similar peers for which to strive, and once one climbs to the top of the similar peers' comparisons, there is still more to attain if one compares a school's score to the standards of exemplars of excellence. This continual striving ensures a results orientation driven by data.

Audience-Based Data

Even the best of data, if incorrectly interpreted, will result in poor or inaccurate conclusions, and these can occur at any and all levels of a school or district. This puts a premium on presenting data in the right ways to the right audiences—the third alignment application of data. Data should enhance recipients' potential to align, not confuse alignment efforts.

Transparency, often held up as a value in regard to data, is sometimes misconstrued to mean "show anyone anything they want to see." We prefer to define transparency as "match the right data to the right purposes for the right audiences." Once that match is determined, fully share the appropriate data.

For example, is the audience internal or external? Internal audiences are comprised of those who make up the three district roles (strategic, tactical, and operational). External audiences are the students who do the learning, the parents who want to know what their children are learning, and community members who want to know if the district is providing something of community benefit. External audiences have their own perspectives, just as do internal audiences. Moreover, both internal and external audiences contain subgroups that will react to the same data differently. In general, consider these factors when using data:

- **Who receives which data is critical**—Sensible, role-based guidelines should be placed around what the district considers to be "data transparency." To cite one obvious example, formative student achievement scores for reading, based on district learning goals and reported by individual student names, should be made available to collaborative teams, but these same data should *not* be made available to members of the board of education, community members, and parents (other than for their own child).

  In this example, transparency guarantees access to those who have a functional need for comprehensive individual student scores (teachers) while withholding it from those who do not (the board and the public).

- **If a data-based culture is to work, it must be safe**—Data must help rather than harm those who are responsible for generating, analyzing, reporting, and making decisions based on those data. In this context, a culture that is not safe is one where data showing unmet goals automatically generates unfair judgment, labeling, discouragement, and punishment. Such an environment drives away the very people who can most positively use data to assist students or plan improvements for the school or district—teachers, administrators, and school leaders.

  However, a safe data environment does not necessarily exclude information that might cause discomfort. Data that inform and make people uncomfortable, without being threatening or intimidating, may be exactly what needs to be heard.

- **Data must align across audiences**—Information needs to align across audiences, even as it is crafted for a particular audience.

  For example, while it is not appropriate to give individual student reading scores to the board or the public, it is appropriate to convert those individual scores to group scores by district, school, or some other large-group cluster, so the board and public can access them in a format that is more aligned to their role-based responsibilities.

  If both the board and the public see reading data that are trending upward overall, for example, the board will be able to assess its overall efforts toward improving achievement levels, and the public will be able to see how successful the district has been in meeting those achievement goals.

- **More data do not mean more clarity**—Absent considerations of audience need and cultural safety, more data are likely to lead to greater confusion. Likewise, providing more data just to satisfy a loosely constructed definition of data transparency will likely produce more misunderstanding than clarity. More data are not necessarily better—*better* data are better. Better data are those that the particular audience can best understand and from which it can gain the most functional benefit. This is accomplished through role-based reporting.

Role-Based Reporting of Data

Data reporting tools, aligned to roles, convert data to audience-specific messages and purposes. In district alignment, we are concerned with two types of data tools—performance scorecards and performance dashboards.

Performance Scorecards

A performance scorecard is to a school or district what a report card is to a student. In a student's report card, the prescribed learning areas are usually listed by subject area (reading, language arts, mathematics, science, social studies, and so on) and, more recently, by standards tied to learning targets. A report card doesn't attempt to give a detailed breakout of how well each student is learning lesson by lesson—that is for teacher conferences, student data folders, artifacts, work samples, and the like. Instead, it attempts to give a big-picture summative view.

A performance scorecard works in a similar fashion, except now the "student" is the school or district. Its data are also summative—they reflect the strategic priorities coupled with measures, and therefore the results are not designed to drive ongoing changes in the short-term. A performance scorecard directly links strategic goals and priorities to measures of those goals and priorities. Because of that linkage, it is the preferred reporting tool at school and district levels.

Let's look at some of the differences between district and school performance scorecards.

A *district performance scorecard* identifies the district's four or five most important strategic priorities; monitors progress toward meeting those priorities through indicators, measures, and targets; and publicly reports results to the district staff and community. Strategic priorities generally address five areas:

1. Student achievement
2. Fiscal health
3. A safe, nurturing learning environment
4. Quality personnel
5. Customer service

The purpose of a district scorecard is not to focus on short- or midterm initiatives or events but on the important, enduring strategic priorities that will *always* be measured. The district scorecard serves as a monitoring instrument for strategists, a resource allocation guide for tacticians, and the primary reporting vehicle to the district's community.

A *school performance scorecard* identifies the same strategic priorities as the district scorecard but does not necessarily use all of the same measures, and certainly not the same targets. It reports on what that school is accomplishing as a subset of what the district is accomplishing.

Using the example of the district long-range strategic SMART goal shown previously (table 2.2, page 16), a district scorecard would report on all students across all schools in the district, using the indicators and measures shown. The school scorecard would report on all students within a single school, aligned to the same indicators and measures on the district scorecard. Individual school scorecards will vary from those of other schools, because schools often add additional indicators and measures for their own analyses. But every school is accountable to the district for the common indicators and measures found in the district scorecard. (See also figs. 5.1 and 5.2, pages 99–101, for examples of district and school scorecard displays.)

Like the district scorecard, the school scorecard is shared with the public as well as the school staff, the board of education, and the central office administration.

Performance Dashboards

Collaborative teams must regularly analyze both summative and formative assessment data from students to know if those students are learning what they need to learn. Team performance dashboards capture student-based assessment data used for a collaborative team's analysis of learning progress.

Team performance dashboards, in our context, becomes a generic term for any collection vehicle for team data. This makes a team performance dashboard a far less prescribed document than a scorecard. However, what a dashboard looks like is not nearly as important as the data contained within it—and whether those data give teams the information they need to make frequent, informed decisions about how to address student learning needs.

Teams have two kinds of data they need to analyze: *summative* data aligned to school and district scorecard results and *formative* data required by teachers to analyze the learning of students before summative assessments occur. A team needs to spend the majority of its analysis time on formative data, which power day-to-day instructional choices and student learning options. But teams also need to understand, through the summative data, how their efforts align with the school and district's efforts to improve learning. (The issue of time spent by collaborative teams on data gathering versus data analysis is a critical one and is addressed in more detail in chapter 5, pages 105–106 and again on page 116.)

The team performance dashboard therefore represents a key operational reporting tool. A grade-level or department performance dashboard is the most important monitoring tool of all, because its measures are so close to the point of impact: student learning in classrooms.

The team performance dashboard is at the center of the generation of common point-of-impact data that can flow throughout the system. This is because data from the team performance dashboard should drive the data reported in the performance scorecards.

This approach represents a significant shift in the way most districts use data. Typically, a strategic analysis of district-level data drives initiatives that affect what teachers are to do next without accounting for what is actually occurring in classrooms.

Formative dashboard data are generated from artifacts such as products or samples of student work collected by collaborative teams. During a workshop in Schaumburg, Illinois, DuFour, DuFour, and Many (2007) discussed the definition of an *artifact*, stating that artifacts may be:

1. Results from common assessments presented to each teacher

2. Analysis sheets indicating team conclusions and strategies for improvement

3. An explanation and analysis of student achievement data from the past two years.

All collaborative teacher teams must produce these operational artifacts.

Collaborative teams also need to collect data on their own work. A team's reflection on its own practices, behaviors, norms, commitments, structures, and processes produces a set of data by which to measure the success of both collaboration and communication at team levels.

Unlike district and school performance scorecards, a grade-level or department dashboard is *not* a public document. Its intended audience is the grade-level or department team and the school's principal. Its function is to provide data that show evidence of the team's data analysis, instructional planning, and improved student achievement.

School and district performance dashboards, like team dashboards, are private reports designed for analysis by principals and district administrators; they go beyond scorecard reports. Typically, such dashboards are more customized in format and include deeper and more specific breakouts of data. Nonetheless, performance dashboards at team, school, or district levels need to align to common districtwide and schoolwide indicators.

There is no classroom performance dashboard or portfolio. If, in a professional learning community, collaborative teams are to be collectively responsible for the learning progress of all students, it becomes counterintuitive to have an individual teacher-based reporting document on student achievement. However, there is a version of a performance dashboard for students—a *student data folder*.

Teachers can use student data folders to compile each student's products, formative and summative assessment results, measurable learning improvement goals set by the student, and charts and graphs on which the student tracks his or her learning progress.

Each student demonstrates responsibility for his or her own learning by maintaining and updating the student data folder. Usually, the data folder is viewed only by that student's teachers and the student. Students who can successfully "walk" their parents through their student data folders at conference times show strong evidence of taking responsibility for their own learning.

Student data folders also have the virtue of alleviating the burden of gathering and formatting a student's learning results. No longer do teachers have to assume all the responsibility of managing a student's record of learning progress. Students, we are finding out, can do a good portion of that themselves. Older students, obviously, have the skills to do more, but younger students can handle a surprising amount when data-folder expectations are aligned to their skill sets.

Scorecards, Dashboards, and Indicators

What makes this scorecard/dashboard sequence effective is that even though indicators and measures for dashboards are strategically set districtwide, the targets vary from scorecard to dashboard, flowing up from operationalists rather than down from strategists. The scorecard/dashboard sequence aligns data across all levels, ensuring that everyone is aiming in the same direction from the same data-based conclusions.

In order for data from team performance dashboards to drive school and district scorecard targets, however, there must be common indicators and measures present in all scorecard and dashboard reporting tools.

As an example, turn to chapter five, figures 5.1–5.3 (pages 99–102). There, a high school math department dashboard (fig. 5.3) reports on all students within the department and is aligned to the same indicators and measures found on the district and school scorecards (figs. 5.1 and 5.2). A third-grade dashboard (not shown) would report on all third-grade students in the school and would be aligned to the indicators and measures on the district scorecard appropriate for third grade. Grade-level or department dashboards must have the same indicators and measures as the school and district scorecards. They can, however, add indicators and measures that are more formative—that more directly inform the team's day-to-day progress monitoring.

So the alignment pattern among scorecards and dashboards is as follows:
1. The district scorecard determines common indicators based on strategic priorities, usually flowing from a strategic plan. Common indicators and key districtwide measures are determined top-down.
2. The school scorecards and team dashboards include those common district indicators and measures.
3. The team dashboards, through data generated by the team, generate targets, which are tied to indicators, designed to improve the team's most recent summative results.
4. The schools and district set their targets based on team targets. Targets are determined bottom-up.

In this fashion, strategic priorities determine areas of districtwide focus, but team data determine targets at all levels of the district.

Table 2.3 (page 24) illustrates aligned reporting tools at six levels of a typical district, accounting for both internal and external audiences.

Table 2.3: Data Aligned Across School District Levels

Level	Student	Classroom	Grade/ Subject Area	School/ Public	District/ Public	Board/ Public
Data Tools	Student data folder	Artifacts, products	Grade / department performance dashboard	School performance scorecard	District performance scorecard (tactical version)	District performance scorecard (strategic version)
Data Distributions	Individual student data	Individual student data by classroom	Student scores across grade or subject area	Student score averages; ranges by grade, subject area, demographics	District score averages/ ranges by grade, subject area; district demographics; schools	District score averages by clustered grades, subject area; district demographics
Data Purpose	Increase one's learning	Inform classroom instruction; monitor student, classroom, team goals progress	Share instructional strategies; monitor classroom, team, school goals progress	Monitor school goals progress	Align resources to learning needs	Monitor strategic goals progress; report to community

Adapted from Van Clay & Soldwedel (2009), The School Board Fieldbook. *Used with permission.*

Applying Loose and Tight Leadership

We have looked at two of the essential elements for alignment: district roles and communicating through data. The next essential element for alignment is loose and tight leadership as it applies to schools and districts.

Loose and tight leadership is based on the premise that relying exclusively on either a tight "top-down" or a loose "bottom-up" leadership approach is not effective. Fullan (2009) has said: "Top-down change doesn't work because it fails to garner ownership, commitment, or even clarity about the nature of reform. Bottom-up change—so-called let a thousand flowers bloom—does not produce success on any scale. A thousand flowers do not bloom and those that do are not perennial." The implication is that a balance between loose and tight provides an optimum leadership style. Of course, getting that balance consistently right is the challenge.

According to DuFour, DuFour, Eaker, and Many (2006), in simultaneous loose and tight leadership "leaders encourage autonomy and creativity (loose) within well defined parameters and priorities that must be honored (tight)" (p. 218).

Richard DuFour (2003, p. 13) gives greater specificity to this loose and tight balance as it applies to professional learning communities:

> We must be "tight" on the fundamental purpose of the organization (learning) and a few big ideas—insisting that those within the organization act in ways consistent with those concepts and demanding that the district align all of its practices and programs with them. . . . [We must] encourage individual and organizational autonomy in the day-to-day operations of the various schools and departments [within the school district]. This autonomy is not character-ized by random acts of innovation, but rather by carefully defined parameters that give focus and direction to schools and those within them.

Peters and Waterman (2004) strike a similar chord: "Organizations that live by the loose-tight principle are, on the one hand, rigidly controlled. Yet at the same time they allow (indeed, insist on): autonomy, entrepreneurship, and innovation from the rank and file" (p. 318).

It is clear from the above literature samples that a combination of loose and tight is required for effective school and district leadership. The trick is in accurately determin-ing an effective balance between the two.

We next look at three indicators of loose and tight as they apply to PLC leadership: (1) reciprocal accountability, (2) role expertise, and (3) commitment to the big ideas.

Reciprocal Accountability

Reciprocity is a key indicator of alignment. Susan Fuhrman and Richard Elmore (2004) write:

> Accountability must be a reciprocal process. For every increment of perfor-mance I demand from you, I have an equal responsibility to provide you with the capacity to meet that expectation. Likewise, for every investment you make in my skill and knowledge, I have a reciprocal responsibility to demon-strate some new increment in performance. (p. 294)

Reciprocal accountability requires that the board of education and superintendent (stra-tegic) be willing to commit the necessary resources—time, materials, and training—to support successful implementation if they expect principals (tactical) and teachers (operational) to embrace a PLC approach. If they do, then it is reasonable to expect teachers to make corresponding changes in classroom instruction, collaborative team-ing, and data analysis, and to focus on improving learning for all students.

Reciprocal accountability is also a counterweight to the cascading effect. If the cascad-ing effect explains why people are so reluctant to change their role perspectives, recip-rocal accountability identifies what changes need to occur and what conditions are required for them to become willing to do so. When all three roles—strategic, tactic, and operational—address the same common messages, districtwide reciprocal account-ability is most likely to occur.

Role Expertise

Role expertise is another indicator of alignment. In an aligned district, strategists act as long-range visionaries, tacticians act as planners and resource allocation specialists, and operationalists who carry out the visions and plans act as student instruction experts. Because districtwide alignment to a professional learning community requires common long-range vision, practical planning, and sound instructional skills, PLCs require blended expertise from all three roles (Van Clay & Soldwedel, 2009).

Look again at table 2.1 (page 15). The cascading effect gives rise to a series of reciprocal responsibilities for each role. Combined, these show an aligned "tight" purpose. The activities performed by expert strategists and expert tacticians support the activities of expert operationalists—reciprocal accountability in action.

The blending of role expertise also meets Fullan, Bertani, & Quinn's (2004) requirement for "widely dispersed leadership." Role expertise translates to leadership opportunities for all three roles, but though leadership may be widely dispersed through its sources, it should always be closely aligned in its impacts.

Commitment to the Big Ideas

There are certain things everyone must commit to doing well across the entire district in order for it to be an effective professional learning community. To use loose and tight language, these are the things that must be absolutely tight. Throughout this book, we use the term *non-negotiable* to describe these practices and policies. The purpose behind non-negotiables is to establish clarity around common expectations at every level of the district. *Non-negotiables* may seem too strong a term for some, connoting the opposite of the collaborative culture championed by professional learning communities. However, a softer word would be misleading. Without non-negotiables, the result could be loose, aimless, and disconnected actions.

For Marzano and Waters (2009), non-negotiables address student achievement and classroom instruction. The implication is that student learning won't improve unless everyone commits to using the same research-proven instructional and achievement-based practices. In this book, we extend Marzano and Waters's notion of non-negotiables to each of the three big ideas of a PLC—ensuring a focus on learning, building a collaborative culture, and establishing a results orientation.

Figure 2.1 identifies the non-negotiables for each of the three big ideas.

All the non-negotiables are necessarily aligned to one another in integrated and simultaneous ways. For example, a guaranteed and viable curriculum provides the essential learning targets, so those who are using a balanced and coherent system of assessment know what to assess. Likewise, a schoolwide pyramid of interventions requires sound data by which to accurately determine what intervention is needed for which student.

answers the first critical question of a PLC: what should each student learn? Because it defines and communicates what each student is expected to know and be able to do, this non-negotiable is foundational to a PLC.

A guaranteed and viable curriculum is standard across the district, equally available to all students, tied to essential learning goals, aligned to state standards, and articulated vertically throughout the district. Without this non-negotiable in place, nothing connects what is taught to what is learned to what is being assessed.

Table 3.1 (page 32) illustrates the specific responsibilities each role assumes in carrying out this non-negotiable.

Strategic Responsibilities

It is the job of board members and others in the strategic role to endorse and promote the importance of the four critical questions (see page 29) to the entire district and the district's public constituents—students, parents, and community. The board also approves curricular goals aligned to state standards. Using these, administrators and teacher leaders serving in the tactical role can create plans to align the curriculum, establish criteria for a balanced and coherent system of assessment, set learning targets and track student progress, set criteria for needed support, and establish a systemwide expectation that all students will actually receive the curriculum. Note the crucial but limited nature of these strategic responsibilities: to stress standards, criteria, and expectations—all big-picture responsibilities.

Strategists, in short, establish tight criteria around the curriculum, along with the expectation that every student will have access to it. Done right and well, this task translates to cultural imperatives that flow through every level of the district.

Tactical Responsibilities

Tactical responsibilities for a guaranteed and viable curriculum involve the establishment of common learning targets for every student enrolled in the same class, course, or grade level. These are the bridges between the common curriculum and the standards the curriculum is designed to address. Tactical responsibilities also include training and monitoring teachers in the use of the common learning targets and guaranteeing that all students are provided access to the curriculum, which is required to address the learning targets.

While the operational role, through the collaborative work of teacher teams, has the most direct knowledge of student learning, the tactical role must meld all of this teacher knowledge to come up with credible, agreed-upon district learning targets. The targets, generated by the tacticians, come from results that "flow up" from teacher-generated evidence of individual student learning. Only such common districtwide targets will allow all students to be assessed on an equal footing.

Table 3.1: Role Responsibilities for a Guaranteed and Viable Curriculum

Strategic	Tactical	Operational
1. Approve school system curricular goals aligned to state standards and translated into common student learning targets expressed by course, subject, or grade level.	1.1 Establish subject-area essential learning targets that represent what each student should learn as a result of a course, subject, or grade level.	1.1.1 Develop essential learning targets that represent what each student should know and be able to do as a result of a course, subject, or grade level.
		1.1.2 Translate essential learning targets into student-friendly language and provide examples or models of the target.
		1.1.3 Deconstruct essential learning targets to identify prerequisite skills necessary to reach mastery.
		1.1.4 Engage in annual review and revision of essential learning targets.
	1.2 Develop and implement training programs and timelines for teachers to understand and use essential learning targets in their instruction.	1.2.1 Acquire the knowledge, skills, tools, and strategies to translate the goals to common essential learning targets in daily classroom practice.
		1.2.2 Use the knowledge, skills, tools, and strategies in common essential learning targets through unit and daily lesson plans.
		1.2.3 Use the knowledge, skills, tools, and strategies to evaluate the appropriateness of the common essential learning targets.
2. Require equitable access to the guaranteed and viable curriculum for all students.	2.1 Monitor implementation of the guaranteed and viable curriculum to ensure equitable access for all students.	2.1.1 Prioritize and consistently focus instruction on the essential learning targets for all students.
		2.1.2 Exercise professional discretion, informed by learning results and best practices, regarding how to teach the essential learning targets.
		2.1.3 Develop pacing guides to set sequence and pacing of instruction.
		2.1.4 Design and deliver lessons that teach to the essential learning targets.

Tacticians monitor and assess the training required for effectively delivering a guaranteed and viable curriculum. They also determine what is tight and what is loose when it comes to training and use of targets. Examples of tight include, for instance, a requirement that targets have common criteria, such as the SMART goal attributes, or that each new target improve upon what was attained from the previous effort. An example of loose would be that teacher teams are responsible for setting new targets, as long as they are higher than previous results.

A brief description of a first-grade team's collaboration on a writing rubric illustrates this point. Here *tight* refers to a districtwide requirement and *loose* means a team decision, unless otherwise indicated.

Collaboration on a Writing Rubric: Loose and Tight

The writing rubric evolved from a common strategic charge to have a district-wide scoring mechanism by which to assess the writing quality of students (tight). The criteria for the rubric were developed by a district committee of teachers and administrators (loose) rather than being purchased or designed by the central office. Then teams collectively scored the writing samples to standardize (tight) their interpretations of how to use the rubric.

Once scores were determined, teams used the writing results to plan instruction around what students already knew and what still needed to be mastered. The district required that targets for the end of the school year, based on SMART goal criteria, be set by each team to show improvement over last spring's measures (tight). Within that district requirement, the first-grade team set its own target for the end of the school year: that 90 percent of its students would earn either a 3 or a 4 on the rubric (loose). But on its own, the team also decided it wanted to assess student progress through the rubric each trimester, in order to monitor ongoing progress toward meeting the end-of-year target. It determined that it would have a first trimester target of 90 percent of students earning a 2 or better and a second trimester target of 75 percent earning a 3 or better (loose). This would allow the team to gauge its progress toward meeting its end-of-year target (loose).

This example also illustrates how a tight long-term SMART goal (meeting or exceeding the required end-of-year target) generated two loose short-term SMART goals (meeting or exceeding targets of 90 percent at 2+ and 75 percent at 3+). The long-term goal was required by the district but was determined from collective team results; the short-term goals were conceived of and applied by the team to support reaching the long-term goal. The long- and short-term goals were aligned.

Operational Responsibilities

Teachers focus instruction on meeting the common learning targets, which involves, of course, teaching common essential skills and concepts that all students are expected to learn.

In a PLC, teams of teachers develop, translate, and craft the learning targets into student-friendly language and models against which students can compare and assess the quality of their work. Teachers must then deconstruct the learning so they can teach those students who need the prerequisite skills required to meet the targets. Teachers must craft lesson plans that address targets and deliver instruction in ways that help students meet these targets. In addition, teacher teams need to establish pacing guides, since learning times for individual students vary.

All of this requires significant training in how to translate goals into targets that resonate in classrooms with students, how to assess the appropriateness of the targets set, how to craft lesson plans, how to focus instruction on what is most essential, and how to deliver instruction that addresses the targets. Indeed, this work can stand as the foundation for the list of tasks and responsibilities of a highly functioning collaborative team—the focus of the next chapter.

A Balanced and Coherent System of Assessment

The second non-negotiable for ensuring a focus on learning requires a balanced and coherent blend of formative and summative assessments that align to the common learning targets of the guaranteed and viable curriculum. Fullan (2005) observes of assessment for learning that "when done well, this is one of the most powerful high-leverage strategies for improving student learning that we know of" (p. 71).

The purpose behind this non-negotiable is to objectively determine whether or not the guaranteed and viable curriculum is being mastered. A balanced and coherent system of assessment answers the second critical question of a PLC: how will we know when each student has learned it? Data from these assessments can be used to diagnose, prescribe, and modify instruction, calibrate the pace of instruction, create entrance and exit criteria for interventions, and identify opportunities for extension and enrichment. Everyone—no matter his or her role—needs to work together to generate accurate, accessible, and valid data at the right time and for the right people in the teaching and learning process.

A balanced and coherent system of assessment should not be mistaken for a results-orientation emphasis (chapter 5). In a results orientation, as we shall see, the emphasis is on how results are used. Here the emphasis is on establishing a *system* of assessments that will produce the results.

Table 3.2 illustrates the specific responsibilities each role assumes in carrying out an aligned, balanced, and coherent system of assessment.

Another important tactical responsibility is to support teachers' efforts to use data at the operational level. Finding time for teams to do this work during the school day is one of the most important ways a principal can provide teachers with tactical support. Specifically, principals should continually create designated and protected time during the day for teams to examine the validity and reliability of their assessments, to analyze the data they produce, and to make the necessary plans to adjust instruction accordingly.

Table 3.2: Role Responsibilities for a Balanced and Coherent System of Assessment

Strategic	Tactical	Operational
3. Require that all assessments be linked to essential learning targets.	3.1 Ensure a balance between formative and summative common assessments to guide instruction during the learning process and reflect on student growth and achievement.	3.1.1 Develop a systematic process to align common formative and summative assessments to essential learning targets and state learning standards. 3.1.2 Know the purpose for which each common formative and summative assessment is to be used. 3.1.3 Participate in the development or selection of common formative and summative assessments. 3.1.4 Secure or create valid and reliable common formative and summative assessments. 3.1.5 Match the method of assessment to the essential learning target.
	3.2 Require an assessment schedule so all stakeholders know when common assessments will be administered, reviewed, and reported.	3.2.1 Schedule dates for administration of common formative and summative assessments. 3.2.2 Schedule dates for reviewing and reporting results of common formative and summative assessments.
4. Ensure the use of a balanced and coherent system of assessment to drive curricular and instructional decisions about student learning.	4.1 Monitor implementation of a balanced and coherent system of assessment to ensure the appropriate locus of control for each category of assessment.	4.1.1 Utilize appropriate formative assessment practices at the classroom level. 4.1.2 Utilize common formative assessment practices at the team and building level. 4.1.3 Utilize common summative assessment practices at the team, building, and district levels. 4.1.4 Utilize appropriate summative assessment practices, reflecting state and national results, at the team, building, and district levels.

continued →

Strategic	Tactical	Operational
4. Ensure the use of a balanced and coherent system of assessment to drive curricular and instructional decisions about student learning. *(continued)*	4.2 Monitor the frequency of use for each category of assessment in a balanced and coherent system of assessment.	4.2.1 Utilize classroom assessment practices on a daily basis. 4.2.2 Utilize common assessment practices every two to four weeks. 4.2.3 Utilize benchmark assessment practices on a quarterly or trimester basis. 4.2.4 Utilize external assessment practices on an annual basis.
	4.3 Ensure that the data generated by each category of assessment is utilized for its appropriate purpose.	4.3.1 Utilize data from classroom assessment practices for the diagnosis and prescription of the learning needs of individual students. 4.3.2 Utilize data from common assessment practices to measure the progress of groups and individual students. 4.3.3 Utilize data from benchmark assessment practices to measure the achievement of groups and individual students. 4.3.4 Utilize data from external assessment practices to identify the greatest areas of need in comparison to others, using state and national comparatives.
	4.4 Monitor the implementation of a balanced and coherent system of assessment to ensure that evidence generated within each assessment category is utilized at the appropriate level of the organization for the appropriate purpose.	4.4.1 Utilize data generated by classroom assessments to demonstrate students' understanding of individual strategies and skills. 4.4.2 Utilize data generated by common assessments to demonstrate students' progress through the curriculum. 4.4.3 Utilize data generated by benchmark assessments to demonstrate students' mastery of the curriculum.

Strategic	Tactical	Operational
4. Ensure the use of a balanced and coherent system of assessment to drive curricular and instructional decisions about student learning. (continued)	4.4 (continued)	4.4.4 Utilize data generated by external assessments to demonstrate the effectiveness of the curriculum and instructional programs.
	4.5 Monitor the implementation of a balanced and coherent system of assessment to ensure that feedback generated by each assessment category triggers the appropriate response by the school and district.	4.5.1 Utilize diagnostic feedback from classroom assessments to guide the reteaching and regrouping of students. 4.5.2 Utilize descriptive feedback from common assessments to facilitate the access to a systematic pyramid of interventions. 4.5.3 Utilize entrance and exit criteria from district benchmark assessments to support ongoing and targeted remedial programs. 4.5.4 Utilize the rank order from the external assessments to provide districtwide comparability and accountability at the classroom level.
5. Ensure the use of an aligned common summative assessment system to report student growth and achievement at the end of the learning process.	5.1 Implement and monitor the use of common summative assessments.	5.1.1 Use common annual assessments to determine student progress toward meeting adequate yearly progress targets, determine program and course effectiveness aligned to the common learning targets, and compare results with like or highest-performing groups. 5.1.2 Eliminate common assessments that do not use data to monitor or report progress related to mastery of common student learning targets or state standards.

Principals also ensure that the arrangement and accessibility of data for teacher teams are accomplished. When teacher teams are forced to load data into a spreadsheet for later analysis, the time lost wastes their expertise and slows the team's planning processes. This all-too-common practice is one of the poorest uses of teachers' time. Technology or clerical aides are far better choices for this turnaround task.

Strategic Responsibilities

Strategic responsibilities for a balanced and coherent system of assessment involve promoting broad expectations that flow from the four critical questions of learning (page 29).

Among the most important expectations are the development and districtwide use of common formative and summative assessments, their alignment to essential learning targets that align to state standards, and the close alignment of those to the district's guaranteed and viable curriculum. Everything aligns to everything else. In short, the strategic responsibility of this second non-negotiable is to insist that this high level of alignment occur in practice districtwide.

Assessments must provide good diagnostic information by which to guide ongoing instruction and good information on whether the planned instruction was successful or needs further modifications (both formative). They must also determine whether the desired learning at the end of instruction actually took place (summative). Although strategists are aware that there are a variety of purposes for assessments, they delegate the actual development of assessments to tacticians and operationalists.

Tactical Responsibilities

The criteria for balancing between formative and summative assessments, as well as the criteria for the assessments themselves, are a tactical responsibility, although one that should be heavily operationally informed.

Many schools and districts rely too much on summative assessments and too little on formative assessments. Standardized summative instruments are easier to obtain and their data easier to collect, but they should not drive instruction. *Formative assessments drive instruction.* Summative assessments report on the results of instruction.

Equally important, all formative and summative assessments must align to each other, to what is being taught, and to whatever data are being collected and analyzed. Tacticians help this alignment by establishing clear understandings of the assessment process. Each assessment should serve a specific and necessary purpose. Together, all assessments should paint a comprehensive picture on which to base instructional decisions. Safeguarding the alignment of assessment is a crucial tactical responsibility.

The need for a quick data turnaround is real. Data from assessments can get stale if not returned to teachers in a timely and organized way. Setting up a system for doing so is a tactical responsibility.

Finally, a critical monitoring and reporting task of those at the tactical level, and of principals in particular, is to continually challenge teacher teams to address student learning based on evidence generated from their assessment data. Principals should model the use of different kinds of data in faculty meetings and with team leaders when communicating with individual teams and teachers; they must also become effective at appropriately confronting those who do not use formative and summative assessment data.

Operational Responsibilities

At the operational level, teachers develop their formative and summative assessments collaboratively, within stated strategic and tactical parameters. They focus on creating assessments that generate data beneficial to direct classroom instruction.

The quantity of data is not the issue. In too many schools, the data teachers have access to have little or no impact on their instructional practices or student learning. In schools aligned to the big ideas of a PLC, everyone acknowledges that teachers are best equipped to write, design, administer, evaluate, analyze, and act upon the results of their formative assessments in guiding their instructional decision making. As assessment becomes more summative, however, the development of the assessments becomes less and less the responsibility of teachers alone and follows a collaborative path between the tactical and operational roles.

All assessment results, formative and summative, need to follow three basic rules: data should be (1) easily accessible, (2) purposefully arranged, and (3) discussed with the proper audiences. Easily accessible data are turned around in a timely fashion to provide results for team dashboards. Purposefully arranged data are presented to teacher teams in ways that are most useful and meaningful to those who must analyze and use those data. The first two rules are tactical responsibilities. Properly discussing the data means sharing those data among the team, so everyone can understand the progress being made, compare the results to best practices and exemplars, adjust ongoing instruction, and provide more time and support for students who have not yet mastered the standards.

The last rule, concerning public discussion, is particularly important and a requirement for the operational work of collaborative teams. The data from common assessments *must* be shared within the team. Then consideration for further sharing and reporting variations of such data can take place. For example, team performance dashboard results might appropriately be shared with a supervising principal, department head, or teaching coach, but not with parents or the community. The former group would understand the formatively diagnostic purpose of such data; the latter audiences would not.

A Schoolwide Pyramid of Interventions

The third non-negotiable for ensuring a focus on learning is establishing a schoolwide pyramid of interventions (see Buffum, Mattos, & Weber, 2009). This non-negotiable answers the third and fourth critical questions of a PLC: How will we respond when a student experiences difficulty in learning? How will we respond to those already proficient? It is the response given to the assessment system data that brings alignment to the guaranteed and viable curriculum.

This third non-negotiable also requires that the learning needs of every student be addressed within the school day. Not every child will master the common learning targets the first time around. Some will have difficulty mastering them at all. Still others will master them quickly but will not be challenged. But all—this is an equity issue—must be challenged to learn at their highest levels, and all—this is an equality issue—must master the guaranteed and viable curriculum, even when the interventions vary from student to student.

As Reeves (2006) observes, "A criterion for schools that have made great strides in achievement and equity is immediate and decisive intervention. . . . Successful schools do not give a second thought to providing preventative assistance for students in need" (p. 87). This non-negotiable requires the district to provide interventions regardless of the time, materials, or instruction required. The only constant here is that *all* children will attain essential learning targets. This non-negotiable is labeled "schoolwide," but that is really shorthand for "systematic and schoolwide," since the entire school must embrace the idea of intervention in an organized and systematic way.

Although each school creates a pyramid of interventions to which all students have equal access, those pyramids may differ from school to school, depending on actual student needs, available resources, and how those resources are used. As one school finds better ways to design the pyramid, others can copy or adapt from it. The schoolwide pyramid of interventions is a focus on learning non-negotiable because it is a strategically tight requirement of the district to meet all students' learning needs. On the other hand, how it is designed and implemented is school-by-school loose—the tactical and operational options emerge from within this tight strategic parameter.

Table 3.3 illustrates the specific responsibilities each role assumes in carrying out an aligned schoolwide pyramid of interventions.

Table 3.3: Role Responsibilities for a Schoolwide Pyramid of Interventions

Strategic	Tactical	Operational
6. Require that a systematic and schoolwide pyramid of interventions be developed and implemented to address the learning needs of *all* students.	6.1 Implement a systematic and schoolwide pyramid of interventions, aligned to the essential learning targets and focused on the common assessment data, to provide extra time and support to those students who have not learned and for those who need additional rigor and challenge.	6.1.1 Design and develop a systematic and schoolwide pyramid of interventions that meets the needs of all students. 6.1.2 Guarantee student access to a schoolwide, systematic pyramid of interventions, regardless of the teacher to whom the student is assigned. 6.1.3 Ensure student access to interventions based on specific expectations of proficiency. 6.1.4 Differentiate time and support for interventions inside the classroom (Tier 1). 6.1.5 Differentiate time and support for interventions outside the classroom (Tiers 2 and 3).

Strategic	Tactical	Operational
6. Require that a systematic and schoolwide pyramid of interventions be developed and implemented to address the learning needs of *all* students. *(continued)*	6.2 Designate protected time during the school day to ensure that interventions are directive rather than invitational.	6.2.1 Identify the students needing interventions. 6.2.2 Ensure that identified students receive the directive interventions. 6.2.3 Deliver interventions during the school day. 6.2.4 Assess the interventions to be certain they make effective use of the designated and protected time.
	6.3 Establish a systematic intervention-monitoring process, with appropriate tools and assessments.	6.3.1 Select appropriate progress-monitoring tools and assessments to assess effectiveness of interventions. 6.3.2 Use common entry and exit criteria aligned to the intervention supports.
7. Provide value-added resources necessary for the system of intervention.	7.1 Request necessary resources, including training, to implement a value-added system of intervention supports.	7.1.1 Request necessary resources—people, time, materials, and training—to implement a value-added system of intervention. 7.1.2 Ensure the systematic schoolwide pyramid of interventions reflects research-based best practices. 7.1.3 Develop skills and expertise in the use of tools, strategies, and processes to maximize the effectiveness of the interventions.

Strategic Responsibilities

Strategic responsibilities for this non-negotiable focus on articulating a common, systemwide vision that the learning needs of *all* students will be addressed and the resources required to make that happen will be provided. This is more complicated than it sounds, because scarce resources have to be prioritized to reflect strategic support for this non-negotiable.

Boards and superintendents promote the importance of a systematic and schoolwide pyramid of interventions by:

- Requiring that clear descriptions of how the pyramids are structured in each school be published to each school community
- Gathering data on the number of students accessing the interventions
- Scheduling public reports from school administrators on the status of the intervention programs
- Ensuring that existing resources are used to support the successful implementation of the pyramids

The resources necessary to support a systematic and schoolwide pyramid of interventions often center on time. Providing time during the school day for additional support may require changes to the daily academic or transportation schedules. This is not how time and other resources are usually allocated in traditional schools, and only those at the strategic level are able to drive these kinds of districtwide changes.

Tactical Responsibilities

There are three tactical responsibilities: (1) to ensure that interventions are systematic and schoolwide, (2) to designate and protect time for interventions, and (3) to monitor an equal access to required interventions for every student.

Creating a systematic and schoolwide pyramid of interventions—more than any other activity—demonstrates a commitment to high levels of learning for all students, not just those who happen to have the right teacher or are serendipitously assigned to the right classroom. The intervention process is also timely, and students are *"required rather than invited"* (DuFour et al., 2010, p. 100, italics added) to utilize the system of time and support.

Principals also have the responsibility to ensure that these interventions are value-added. They need to protect programs that show evidence of improved student learning and cease protecting those that do not. This represents a significant shift in the use of resources. How many district resource priorities would remain so if the priority litmus test were based squarely on evidence of improved student learning?

Finally, principals are responsible for scheduling designated and protected time for interventions. Designating time during the school day is the best way to meet the requirement that interventions be directive rather than invitational. This doesn't mean that time and support cannot be offered at other times—they should whenever possible—but it does mean that the school is obliged to offer as many interventions as possible when those needing them are available.

Two ways to create protected time for interventions are adjustable schedule blocks and the 9:1 model.

Adjustable Schedule Blocks

Some schools have modified the traditional schedule to accommodate pyramids of intervention during the regular school day.

Consider a secondary school where the schedule consists of nine fifty-minute periods each day: six are for core academics, two for specials or electives, and one for lunch. By taking three minutes from each of the nine periods, principals can create twenty-seven designated and protected minutes for interventions. The restructured schedule still reflects nine periods of forty-seven minutes each. Inserting the additional time immediately before or after the student lunch period creates an effective block of time for systematic and schoolwide pyramids of interventions during the regular school day.

The 9:1 Model

At the elementary level, teachers have used a 9:1 model to create time for intervention. Teams of teachers teach the same unit of instruction for nine consecutive days. On the ninth day of instruction, all students are given a common assessment. The team then gathers together at the end of the ninth day to analyze the results, regroup the students based on those results, and plan ways to differentiate the next day's lessons. Some students receive specific intervention, while others participate in extension and enrichment activities.

Operational Responsibilities

At an operational level, teacher responsibilities center around designing intervention strategies, carrying them out, monitoring their progress, and protecting the time allotted for them. The design of each intervention starts and ends with identifying the specific learning needs of individual students. As mentioned, this is a data-driven process, dependent largely on the results generated by common assessments in classrooms and analyses by collaborative teams.

The interventions themselves are then collaboratively designed and developed by the teams, which is one reason collaborative teams need to stay current with the latest research on learning and best practices. The team then collaboratively divides the interventions among the team members, trying to optimally match teaching strengths to student learning needs.

The monitoring is processed by teams through formative assessment results from two directions. At the front end, early formative results shape the types of intervention content and instructional approaches to be used. At the back end, formative monitoring of results assesses the impact of the intervention and link to the next level of instruction—did student learning improve as a result of the intervention? Was the intervention successful?

While tacticians provide the designated and protected time, operationalists must commit as a team to utilizing that time productively. Planning, carrying out, and monitoring interventions and sharing, as a team, responsibility for the learning of all students can easily feel to teachers like an additional burden, especially when most teachers feel they never have enough time as it is. Ensuring there is an adequate and protected time helps teachers cope with these demands of collaborative work; it also provides directive rather than invitational opportunities for students.

Alignment Constants

The alignment constants for a focus on learning are the same as for the other big ideas:

1. Policies, practices, and procedures

2. Aligned appraisal systems

3. Resources and training

4. Monitoring and reporting

Each strategic responsibility corresponds with one of the four alignment constants for a focus on learning (table 3.4). Specific tactical and operational responsibilities cascade from each of these.

Strategic Responsibilities

In general, the focus on learning alignment constants include strategic responsibilities that center on:

- Setting and aligning districtwide expectations toward a focus on learning (policies, practices, and procedures)

- Requiring that all appraisal systems align to focus on learning non-negotiables (appraisals systems)

- Supplying the financial support for the provision of necessary training and resources required by a focus on learning (resources and training)

- Requiring accountability data on how a focus on learning is being implemented across the school district (monitoring and reporting)

One strategic example from the policies, practices, and procedures constant is to direct the administration to perform an "alignment audit"—identifying policies, practices, programs, and procedures that do *not* align with a focus on learning—and to make appropriate recommendations. This strategic charge to the district's administration forces it to look at improving alignment as one target of ongoing districtwide improvement, in the same way that targets are set for improving student learning.

Table 3.4: Role Responsibilities for the Alignment Constants for Ensuring a Focus on Learning

Alignment Constant	Strategic	Tactical	Operational
Policies, practices, and procedures	8. Require an analysis, by school and district office, of the policies, practices, and procedures that do and do not align with a focus on learning, followed by an action plan for addressing those policies, practices, and procedures that are not aligned.	8.1 Produce a summary, by school and district office, of practices and procedures that do not align with a focus on learning, and create specific recommendations as to what can be done to better align to that end.	8.1.1 Review policies, practices, and procedures that align with a focus on learning. 8.1.2 Celebrate those policies, practices, and procedures that are in alignment, and act on what needs to be changed for those not in alignment.
		8.2 Provide examples of best practice, through literature and experiences, for stakeholders to communicate compelling rationales for making shifts from where we are to where we need to be around a focus on learning.	8.2.1 Ensure that teaching practices are in line with best practice research aligned to a focus on learning. 8.2.2 Examine present practices and procedures by experimenting with doing things differently to get better results.
Aligned appraisal systems	9. Require that district appraisal systems align the non-negotiables for a focus on learning with district standards for performance.	9.1 Ensure that the non-negotiables for a focus on learning are aligned to the performance appraisal feedback systems.	9.1.1 Collect appraisal assessment data, aligned to the non-negotiables for a focus on learning, through self-, peer/team, and supervisor assessment data. 9.1.2 Use appraisal assessment data to establish professional growth plans and actions that lead to improved student and teacher performance.

continued →

Alignment Constant	Strategic	Tactical	Operational
Appraisal systems *(continued)*		9.2 Use non-negotiables for a focus on learning to guide recruitment, selection, induction, retention, mentoring, and professional growth.	9.2.1 Provide input into the recruitment and selection of new staff against the non-negotiables for a focus on learning. 9.2.2 Mentor others to develop capacity to deploy and sustain the non-negotiables for a focus on learning.
Resources and training	10. Align resources for support and training to ensure systematic (collaborating horizontally within roles) and systemic (collaborating vertically across roles) deployment of the non-negotiables for a focus on learning.	10.1 Provide opportunities to learn, apply, and reflect on best practices aligned to the non-negotiables for a focus on learning.	10.1.1 Participate in professional development to reflect on practice and gain additional tools, skills, strategies, and knowledge to meet district expectations for focus on learning non-negotiables. 10.1.2 Assist colleagues in meeting district expectations for focus on learning non-negotiables.
		10.2 Promote an ongoing expectation that administrators will model and teachers will expect a continual study and sharing of best practices, aligned to a focus on learning.	10.2.1 Participate as an active, contributing member of a team that commits to regular and continual study and the sharing of instructional and learning best practices to ensure a focus on learning. 10.2.2 Identify changes in practices that link to measurably improved results.

Alignment Constant	Strategic	Tactical	Operational
Monitoring and reporting	11. Require at each level of the system—student, classroom, team/department, school, program, and district—that improvement efforts, through deployment of non-negotiables for a focus on learning, are monitored and reported.	11.1 Monitor system requirements through agenda planning and focused discussion to assess progress related to focus on learning non-negotiables.	11.1.1 Examine teaching and learning results to see if improvements are being made based on focus on learning non-negotiables. 11.1.2 Share strategies to further guide improvement or redirect improvement efforts. 11.1.3 Track progress through data charts, graphs, or logs.
		11.2 Report system requirements to stakeholders through scheduled communication processes.	11.2.1 Share results through clear communication processes and reporting tools. 11.2.2 Reflect both formatively and summatively on results to be certain improvement efforts are adding value.

Tactical Responsibilities

Tactical responsibilities, such as the following, spin off from the strategic responsibilities for each of the alignment constants.

1. The administration performs a review and crafts recommendations for improving alignment around a focus on learning. The completed audit will drive future alignment efforts across the district.

2. The administration also plans for shifts from where the district is to where the district wants to be. The district will have the same improvement indicators driving each level of the system. One way to accomplish this is to model an expectation that a continual study of best practices become the norm for all. This means that district administrators and principals have to stay current and informed in best instructional practices, so they can model the importance of staying current to teachers. This is not a responsibility that tacticians can effectively delegate to someone else.

3. If a school district is committed to ensuring a focus on learning, an aligned appraisal system should reflect that focus. If the district is measuring data linked to essential benchmarks of student learning, the appraisal system for the district's professionals should translate to responsibilities at the strategic, tactical, and operational levels that align to the achievement data.

4. The administration is responsible for providing the quality controls for what is considered best practice and access to training, examples, and literature, and for establishing common messages, expectations, and professional language for the entire district.

5. Another pair of tactical responsibilities involves monitoring and reporting on the implementation throughout the district of the non-negotiables for ensuring a focus on learning by utilizing the school and district performance scorecards discussed in chapter 2 (pages 19–23).

Operational Responsibilities

At an operational level, the responsibility of teachers is to embed a focus on learning into their everyday practices and responsibilities. They do this in at least six ways:

1. Providing "on the ground" reflection on policies, practices, and procedures
2. Continually referencing best practices for ideas and corrections
3. Using data to improve performance
4. Mentoring each other to improve individual and group practices
5. Committing to ongoing collaborative study and reflection
6. Consistently contributing as a value-added member of the collaborative team

As one example, the policy reflections require an operational "reality check" on the procedures and practices that the district embraces. Teachers are not asked to challenge the district's mission, vision, values, and goals, but they are asked to reflect on the impact that supports, resources, and materials are having on improving student learning. These teacher-based reflections are about getting operational feedback on how strategic goals and tactical plans are changing things on the ground—in the classroom. Such reflections align all three roles by gathering information from each area of expertise toward a common vision.

The reliance on staying current on best practices is what keeps teachers nimble in confronting learning issues. Tacticians can make best practice information available, but operationalists must take responsibility for studying and using it. In a school system committed to ensuring a focus on learning, continuously reflecting on one's own practices becomes an operationalist's professional obligation.

In a similar fashion, aligned appraisal feedback also presents teachers with learning of their own. Here again, information is being provided to help people become better in their practice.

A commitment to mentoring is a commitment to the idea that "we are all in this together" and have a professional obligation both to help others improve and to learn from one another. Team members can create opportunities in which this can occur.

Study and self-reflection are commitments to the notion that a teacher has responsibility for her or his own learning, as do the students. New learning does not come already packaged; one must commit to seeking it out on one's own. This is where team members take on individual learning roles beyond whatever the school or district is providing.

Finally, contributing as an active, value-added member of the collaborative team is also a professional obligation for a focus on learning. One must accept that one can learn more in collaboration with others than individually, that the team is there for support rather than to make critical judgments, that all members of the team have a common purpose in improving every student's learning, and that the team can provide resources and ideas so problems do not have to be faced or solved alone.

Aligning these commitments to an appraisal system's standards for performance is critical. Providing feedback and support to ensure effective deployment of those standards is the engine that drives continuous improvement.

Case Study for a Focus on Learning

This following story illustrates how a focus on learning was presented in the fictional Nirvana district—with very mixed results. It describes what went seriously wrong with initial attempts to implement a strategic plan to establish PLCs across the district. After telling the story, we will deconstruct it to find out why those attempts failed. Actions from all three roles—strategic, tactical, and operational—are illustrated.

A Focus on Learning Gets Derailed

The previous spring, the district had gathered parents, members of the faculty and staff, students, and administration for a three-day visioning conference. One of the goals had been to ensure high levels of learning for all, and the board had adopted the professional learning community model as one of the key strategies in its long-range strategic plan.

During its goal-setting process the following summer, the board identified the implementation of PLCs as a primary district goal and directed Superintendent Sue Stanfield to make implementing PLCs one of her top priorities.

Among the dozens of three-ring binders on her office shelves was a plan she had developed to respond to the board's strategic charge. Sue had spent hours working alone in her office and was very proud of the plan. She designated PLCs as the topic for the opening institute day and directed each of the principals to design a one-day workshop focusing on the four critical questions for a focus on learning.

At the first administrative council meeting in early August, each principal was given the same three-ring binder, which laid out the district's strategic plan for the school year. The plan identified learning objectives, timelines, and speakers for each of the institute days from September to June. Once again, each principal was reminded of his or her responsibility to develop a school plan for the opening institute day, the purpose of which was to introduce the four critical questions of a focus on learning.

Later that month, the faculty of a Nirvana magnet high school for the arts had gathered together for its opening institute. The students at this school were all gifted artists, dancers, and musicians. Likewise, the teachers were gifted artists in their own right. The focus of the school was on helping these students maximize their significant artistic talents. The magnet school's principal, Gail Sweeney, was a veteran educator as well as an accomplished musician, who regularly performed as a soloist in her church choir and was active in local community theater musicals.

Gail thought the first portion of the morning had gone very well, but just before the mid-morning break, Mary Lancroft, a veteran member of the faculty and a long-time vocal music teacher, stood and shouted from the back of the room, "I've had enough! It's PLC this and PLC that. All I ever hear about is PLC. If you take the L out of PLC, all you're left with is 'PC'—I've never been politically correct in my life, and I'm not starting now!" Since Mary was obviously agitated and upset with the morning's conversation, Gail deviated from the meeting agenda to ask Mary to explain why she felt as she did.

"I'm tired of listening to how I have to change what I do," Mary said. "I'm a good teacher, and I work hard. I don't understand why I have to totally change everything I've been doing very successfully for the past twenty years."

Gail decided to reframe the conversation. "Mary, you've taught here for a long time, and your students have been very successful. Let me ask you, are there certain things your students need to know and be able to do to be successful in your music class?" Mary responded with a litany of musical terminology and performance techniques that she expected all of her students to be able to demonstrate.

Mary was very, very clear about her expectations for what her students should learn; she was also very, very clear about why she wanted her students to learn the outcomes before they left her class. Without knowing it, Mary had just answered question #1 of a PLC—what do we want each student to learn?

Gail continued, "That's great, but how do you know the students have mastered those concepts?" Mary went on to describe a comprehensive set of performance assessments in which every student had participated. The performance assessments were specific to the common learning targets the district had agreed all students must learn.

It was obvious that Mary had a firm grasp of strategies she could use to confirm whether or not her students understood the concepts of skills she expected. Again, without realizing it, Mary had articulated the answer to question #2 of a PLC—how do we know when each student has learned it?

Although the tension in the room remained high, Gail pushed on and asked, "Mary, do all the students get it? I mean, what happens when some of the kids need more help to be successful? And what do you do for the kids who get it quickly? Is there anything that you do to push them further along?"

A little exasperated, Mary explained that she came in early, stayed late, and often worked through lunch—and even an occasional Saturday—to help students prepare for their auditions. She also routinely increased the sophistication of the audition selections for those who could handle something more demanding. Once again, she knew the answers, this time to questions #3 and #4 of a PLC—how will we respond when a student experiences difficulty in learning, and how will we extend learning for those who have already learned the essentials?

Although Mary understood good teaching and had obviously just demonstrated that she understood the critical questions, her lack of familiarity with the language used to describe them prevented her understanding what the principal was talking about.

Seeing that Mary had a firm grasp of what and how she was teaching, Gail asked, "How about for the rest of the day, we just call this work 'best practices.' Are you OK with that?" To which Mary harrumphed, "Fine," and sat down.

Gail completed the rest of the institute day agenda and went back to her office once the teachers were dismissed. She pulled out the superintendent's beautiful three-ring binder and reviewed the plan for the year. Gail saw immediately that there was no time for teachers to reflect on their practices, build shared knowledge, or come to agreement on what terminology they would use when discussing teaching and learning. She sensed an impending disaster unless the plan was tweaked to allow more time for teachers to talk together.

The next meeting of the administrative council focused on a debriefing of the opening institute day, but when Gail shared her experience of the previous day and suggested that some time be set aside solely for the purpose of building a common PLC vocabulary, Sue Stanfield rebuffed the suggestion of any change in plans. Even after principals from several other buildings mentioned similar concerns, she closed the door to any further conversation, stating, "This plan has already been approved by the board of education" and suggested that the principals "find some courage and fast!"

Deconstructing the Story: What Went Right

One does not have to be overly prescient to see where this story is headed. Even though it was clearly the right goal, the establishment of PLCs across the district is not likely to be successful in this instance unless certain roles make some fundamental changes in behavior.

That doesn't mean that nothing was done appropriately. Let's first look at what was done right, and by which role.

Strategic

- A three-day collaborative visioning conference represented a sound strategic planning base. The wide representation strengthened the likelihood of support later on, and the visioning task kept everyone strategic rather than tactical or operational.

- A broad-based strategic goal gave clear visionary direction to the school system while still leaving plenty of flexibility for implementation decisions.

- The board's adoption of the PLC approach was its first appropriately tight strategic decision, giving further clarity of focus and purpose to the school system.

- It was strategically appropriate for the board to assign the planning of the PLC goal to the superintendent and her staff rather than attempting to micromanage that planning itself.

Tactical

- The superintendent was correct in responding to the board's PLC commitment and taking such a charge seriously. But, as we saw by the story's outcome, it was *how* she responded that ultimately made all of the difference.

- Discussion around the four critical questions was an excellent way to establish the importance of a focus on learning.

- The charge to principals to develop a school plan to address the four critical questions was a good mix of tight and loose: tight in that the parameters for the school institutes were clear (four critical questions, focus on learning) but loose in that the design of how to address those parameters was left to the principals.

- A debriefing by the superintendent as to how the various school institute days went was a sound next step—*if* the feedback that emerged had been actually considered.

- By giving the music teacher time to explain her frustrations rather than responding in kind, the principal showed respect for her while still continuing a focus on the four critical questions.

- By pushing on, even with tension in the room, the principal determined that a chance at a teachable moment was more important than avoiding the tension.

Yet in the way the principal calmly and respectfully dialogued with a frustrated teacher, it was clear that she cared about feelings in the room.

- The music teacher answered the third and fourth critical questions as thoroughly as she had the previous two, offering excellent examples for the principal to use.

- When the principal couldn't get the music teacher to adapt to the PLC language, she allowed her to stand on language she did understand that meant the same thing. This defused the teacher's anger for the rest of the meeting.

Operational

- The notion of "best practices" was inserted into the institute discussion, and even the music teacher conceded, in different words, that the four critical questions were valid instructional considerations.

- Just because the music teacher couldn't express herself in PLC language didn't mean she wasn't already practicing sound instructional principles.

- The music teacher was able to clearly articulate exactly how she utilized performance assessments to determine what her students had learned.

Deconstructing the Story: What Went Wrong

Let's look at specifically what went wrong, again according to role.

Strategic

- Because the superintendent decided only she could "own" the implementation plan, the first big opportunity for collaboration around a focus on learning was lost.

- The language of PLCs confused rather than enlightened good teachers like the music teacher. Teachers often confuse new language with new responsibilities and think the new responsibilities—no matter how worthy—are just "more things on my plate."

- The superintendent's plan apparently did not allow for changes and adjustments based on feedback from those either training or receiving the training.

- The fact that there were already dozens of three-ring binders on the superintendent's shelf suggests a lack of ongoing leadership focus. Will this PLC initiative be something that is sustained over time or will it become simply one more initiative in a continuous line of "next new things"?

- By stating, "This plan has already been approved by the board of education," the superintendent confused a strategic charge to implement a plan with the tactical and operational details that the plan must address to succeed.

- A PLC initiative—or any new initiative—should not require that a school like the magnet high school abandon its commitment to its core learning mission—in this case, developing student talents in the arts.

Tactical

- Proud as the superintendent may have been of her plan, spending hours working alone in her office represented a very narrow and noncollaborative approach—a clear violation of the second big idea of a PLC: implementing a collaborative culture.

- By including learning objectives, timelines, and speakers in her plan, the superintendent was micromanaging tactical decisions better suited to central office administrators and principals, aided by teacher input. Requiring these things was strategically appropriate, but determining specifically what they should be was not.

- The magnet high school principal's review of the superintendent's plan exposed the fact that there was no time for teachers to make meaning of the work, including building shared knowledge or coming to agreement on terminology.

- When the superintendent rebuffed any changes in the plan, she was ignoring vital tactical feedback on operational needs. She confused feedback with criticism, thereby dooming the success of her plan, even given adroit communicators like the magnet high school principal.

- By stating, "Find some courage and fast!" the superintendent sent the message to her administrators that input will not be tolerated. This superintendent was missing the loose and tight balance that any good PLC-based plan requires.

Operational

- A common teacher fear was stated clearly and directly when the music teacher said, "I don't understand why I have to totally change everything I've been doing successfully for the last twenty years." For her to embrace this change, she would need to see how the changes align rather than conflict with what she knows she does well.

- If the music teacher had known that what she was already doing is what a focus on learning seeks, she could have become a model for change rather than a vocal critic of it. By not knowing, she risked being an impediment to the very beliefs she practiced.

This story could have had a happy ending if the three district roles had acted in a collaborative fashion to successfully align toward a districtwide focus on learning. Here is how the story might sound replayed with different role behaviors.

Revisiting the Story

The board of education set a strategic vision for the critical question, "What do we want our students to know and be able to do?" by engaging in its annual practice of reviewing the guaranteed and viable curriculum before school began in the fall, thereby demonstrating its critical importance.

The review involved all three roles in the same public conversation, which improved the chances for ownership of a guaranteed and viable curriculum and common learning targets at each level. The initiative that emerged was to establish common formative and summative assessments.

The board, led by Superintendent Sue Stanfield and board finance committee chairperson George Bell, then considered some annual budget priorities to reflect this strategic initiative. Based on the finance committee's resource projections, the board set a goal that a balanced and coherent system of assessment would be successfully implemented over the next three years, and that resources—money, time, and personnel—would be allocated to support that initiative.

The board established the expectation that the entire school system would engage in research-supported assessment practices through an annual goal-setting process. The board also charged Superintendent Sue Stanfield and the administration with setting a few targeted goals with clear outcomes, the only parameters being that they represent essential learning expected of all students and that the targets show improvement over previous years' results. These annual goals—challenging yet attainable—were structured in such a way that their successful implementation could be accomplished only by the staff working interdependently toward a common goal.

The board then charged Sue with planning how to communicate to parents, faculty, and staff the importance to the district's mission and vision of the common assessment initiative. This communications plan was reinforced through a series of quarterly updates and progress reports distributed to the public.

The responsibilities for implementing the common formative assessment initiative fell to the tactically oriented assistant superintendant, Ben Korbett, and the Nirvana principals—not the strategically based Sue Stanfield. Sue's charge to Ben and the principals was to organize a summer writing team of qualified teachers to review and revise the essential outcomes upon which the common formative assessments would be based. Administrators would provide the conditions—time, materials, and training resources—under which the process could be successfully completed.

Ben was also charged with building a rationale for the initiative among principals, other administrators, and the board of education. This first step of building shared knowledge resulted in the creation of a guiding coalition that consistently supported this initiative across all district schools.

Administrators identified teachers to pull together the state and national standards documents, gather existing curriculum guides, and collect appropriate local, state, and national assessment results. The administrators created a schedule, secured a location for the work, and set up the method of compensation, while ensuring that any other materials the teachers may need were available. Then they began to monitor—not micromanage—the work assigned to the teachers.

The detailed planning work began once a solid foundation of shared knowledge was created for those in the tactical role. At this point, commitments were made, plans were developed, budgets allocated, schedules created, and communication strategies put into place. At this critical juncture, the strategic and tactical roles—through the board, the district office administration, and the principals—took extra care to be aligned on the "what" and "why" of the initiative. They knew any lack of understanding or commitment as to what a balanced and coherent system of assessments looks like or why the use of common formative assessments is critical to the success of all students, would doom the initiative.

This also inspired hard conversations among Sue, Ben, principals, teacher leaders, and the board regarding implementation timelines. The board typically wanted to see quick results, but Sue and Ben reminded everyone that a change in assessment practices is complex and takes time. The administration argued that smoother and more lasting progress would occur with a less aggressive timeline and more incremental, measurable progress points along the way.

At the school level, principals assisted in the translation of the strategic initiative to operational language, as did magnet school principal Gail Sweeney. Principals took responsibility for supporting the most practical aspects of the tactical plan, with *practical* meaning most likely to garner teacher support. They also contributed to the plan's success by establishing clear expectations and creating the conditions that would facilitate teacher adoption of common new assessment practices.

Principals also aligned the school resources—time, money, and personnel—to support the use of common assessments. In real time, principals engaged in setting up building schedules, regularly meeting with teacher teams, and consistently monitoring their meetings. Principals communicated the linkage of common formative assessments to the strategic vision of a focus on learning, as put forth by the board. Part of the principals' responsibility was to help teachers understand the "why" behind the change and how the "why" affects them and their teaching day to day.

Principals, supported by district office administrators, confronted those who they felt wanted to ignore or sabotage the initiative, aware that if any teachers were allowed to opt out of using common formative assessments, a consistent focus on learning for all children in the school would be fatally compromised. The tactics for carrying out these meetings were worked out in advance among Sue, Ben, Gail (as the principal's representative), and a teachers' team led by teachers association president Barbara King. The stated purpose of the meetings was not to punish or chastise, but rather to make clear what district non-negotiables around a focus on learning were expected of all.

At the operational level, teams of teachers were charged with the responsibility of updating the essential outcomes each year—the basis for the common formative assessments—through the use of a curriculum framework. To accomplish this, the district would maintain a current standards document, as follows:

1. Suggestions for changes would be gathered from job-alike and/or department meetings held throughout the school year. Curriculum study committees would submit written suggestions based on new adoptions or additional staff training that may have taken place during the year.

2. Each June, teams of teachers would review feedback and suggestions from their colleagues and identify what needed to be revised.

3. At the same time, these teacher teams would review assessment data and look for patterns of student performance, areas of weakness or less-than-satisfactory results, and general trends. All of this practical experience and information would be folded into a new set of curriculum frameworks prepared for the board's consideration each August.

Any changes in essential outcomes would be highlighted and publicly explained to the board in an open meeting. The regular, routine review of the essential outcomes each and every August would send a clear message that the existence of a guaranteed and viable curriculum was non-negotiable.

Summary

As the story showed, it was not enough that the board set forth a clear vision derived from a solid community consensus. Nor was it enough that the magnet school principal was a superb communicator who had a clear understanding of both her staff and what a focus on learning was all about. Moreover, as appropriate and research-based as a focus on learning might be, it alone was not enough to cause staff to embrace and apply it. Teachers will cite not enough time, not enough training, or not enough clarity about what is expected. Some may be confused about the process of implementing the change or unsure who is responsible for each part of the effort. It is at these points of confusion that tacticians need to step in. Being confused is a natural state, but staying confused takes effort.

Teachers must have time to reflect on what they are being asked to do—to examine the "how." What was needed here—what is always needed—are the coordinated efforts of the three roles aligned in a districtwide approach toward implementing a focus on learning. Only through an aligned, districtwide approach can the implementation of a focus on learning be universally successful, efficiently implemented, and sustainable across an entire district.

Conclusion

This chapter began by identifying a focus on learning as the brightest star in a PLC constellation, because it describes what is most important in establishing the focus of a professional learning community.

We discussed role-based responsibilities for each of the three non-negotiables for a focus on learning—(1) a guaranteed and viable curriculum, (2) a balanced and coherent system of assessments, and (3) a schoolwide pyramid of interventions. We then examined the impacts of the four alignment constants on a focus on learning.

Next we presented and deconstructed the Nirvana School District's failed attempt to establish a focus on learning and reconstructed the same story to show how a more aligned, districtwide approach could have succeeded.

The next chapter focuses on the role-based responsibilities for the non-negotiables of the second of the three big ideas—a collaborative culture—and uses another Nirvana School District story to illustrate the need for an aligned approach.

chapter four

Aligning to a Collaborative Culture

Great things are not done by impulse, but by a series of things brought together.

—Vincent Van Gogh

It is not enough for teams of teachers to collaborate. The need for alignment among the roles demands the development of a districtwide collaborative culture. This big idea defines what everyone in the system must do well *together*. It defines the systematic (collaborating horizontally within roles) and systemic (collaborating vertically across roles) expectations a school system holds for working together. Collaboration among and between strategic, tactical, and operational roles is therefore required.

Let's look at the basic tasks of all three roles for building a collaborative culture.

The Strategic Role

Strategists must establish the non-negotiables that shape the organization's efforts toward establishing a collaborative culture both within and across district roles. They do this in three ways: (1) by establishing policy; (2) by promoting a shared mission, vision, values, and goals; and (3) by modeling openness to feedback.

Policies serve as statements of visionary or missionary intent—statements the entire district needs to embrace. They provide the unifying message and common language that everyone in the district shares and understands.

The shared mission, vision, values, and goals (one of the non-negotiables in this chapter) are strategically expressed by what everyone in the organization articulates, protects, and promotes. Consistent messages, backed up by resources that promote those messages at tactical and operational levels and by priorities that give them special weight, send powerful statements across every level of a school system. Articulating common messages is a key strategic responsibility.

Modeling openness to tactical and operational feedback doesn't mean that strategic non-negotiables are bargainable. After all, a non-negotiable is just that. Instead, it represents what the district is going to be tight about. The "how" regarding implementation can be looser. Indeed, the establishment of a collaborative culture will need to have some looseness in its application if the notion of collaboration is to have any district-wide credibility.

Strategists also model their openness by guarding against the five mistakes leaders make (DuFour et al., 2008):

- Attempting to "go it alone" (not seeking tactical or operational expertise)
- Using a forum ill-suited to the dialogue necessary for consensus (not accounting for role-based needs or having the wrong role deliver the message)
- Pooling opinion (ignoring role-based expertise and best practices) rather than building shared knowledge
- Allowing ambiguity in the standard for moving forward (a lack of clarity between loose and tight)
- Setting unrealistic standards for moving forward (strategic charges not aligned to tactical and operational abilities and resources)

The Tactical Role

This big idea requires communicators who can effectively build a bridge between the non-negotiables articulated at the strategic level and the operationalists who must be allowed some latitude in implementing them. Being tight about what DuFour et al. (2008) refer to as the "imperatives" of the school system (the equivalent of Marzano and Waters's [2009] "non-negotiable goals") is the accountability piece. Tacticians—at both central office and school levels—are the ones who are responsible for monitoring and enforcing accountability.

On the other hand, tacticians need to deftly blend all of the varied operational talents and resources available in the district and positively channel them into common purposes and practices. This is the collaborative piece, because that blending of talents and resources cannot successfully occur through dictums alone. Tacticians must therefore embody the essence of loose and tight leadership, particularly at the school level.

Openness to discussion is crucial because the three roles, left each to their own, rarely agree on what should be tight. The truth is that if schools wait until the heavens open, angelic harps ripple as a light shines down on the teachers lounge, and everyone is struck with the same understanding in a moment of spontaneous enlightenment, nothing different will ever happen. The expectations around collaboration do not require unanimous agreement, but they do need to be clear, explicitly stated, and practical enough to make operational sense if teachers are to reasonably be expected to carry them out.

The Operational Role

At an operational level, teachers—as a collaborative team—need to make efficient and effective use of time to improve student performance results. Teams accomplish this by carrying out results-oriented discussions around student learning. These discussions and the decisions teams make emerge from the conversations that take place during their designated and protected time together.

This in turn has an impact on long-held and time-honored traditions that are prevalent at the operational level. There is a notion that collaborative team time is taken from a more appropriate use of planning time—an individual teacher's planning. But the expectation that teachers will work together in collaborative teams to ensure that all students learn should not be negotiated. There is no evidence in the literature that teachers working in isolation produce better results than those working collaboratively. Similarly, the ways that collaborative teams organize themselves and document their work (discussed later in this chapter) need not reflect a consensus of all faculty.

Planning time in most schools, in fact, more accurately represents preparation time—typically an isolated act of preparing or gathering the necessary materials, equipment, and supplies for upcoming instruction. This is very different from the collaborative planning that is at the heart of a professional learning community.

In a PLC, planning time is when teachers plan together. During that planning time they collaboratively discuss, analyze, and reflect on all aspects of the teaching and learning process. One simply cannot effectively engage in those kinds of activities in isolation. In a PLC, planning time rarely involves gathering or preparing materials for an upcoming lesson. Instead, planning time allows a team to collectively address the non-negotiables for a focus on learning: a guaranteed and viable curriculum, a balanced and coherent system of assessments, and a schoolwide pyramid of interventions.

This distinction is important. If student learning is the responsibility of the team, it stands to reason that instructional planning will be more effective if it is a shared responsibility of the team as well. This doesn't mean that teachers should not have individual preparation time, but it does mean that collaborative planning needs to be a priority.

Let's look at how each of the non-negotiables plays out, role by role, to align around building a collaborative culture.

Non-Negotiables for Building a Collaborative Culture

There are three non-negotiables for building a collaborative culture: (1) shared mission, vision, values, and goals; (2) high-performing collaborative teams; and (3) intentional collaboration.

Shared Mission, Vision, Values, and Goals

Senge (1990) stresses the importance of a common systemic message in stating, "One is hard pressed to think of any organization that has sustained some measure of greatness in the absence of goals, values, and missions that become deeply shared throughout the organization" (p. 163). Professional learning communities prove Senge's observation through executing the model presented by DuFour et al. (2008). PLCs define each of this first non-negotiable's terms, in the context of being publicly shared, as follows:

- Mission = purpose
- Vision = clear direction
- Values = collective commitments
- Goals = indicators, timelines, and targets

Table 4.1 illustrates the specific aligned responsibilities that each role assumes for shared mission, vision, values, and goals.

Strategic Responsibilities

Clear and concise mission, vision, value, and strategic goal statements center on a focus on learning. Strategically, these statements represent what students, teachers, and administrators together should learn while working collaboratively. Strategists state this non-negotiable as a district policy and lay out a clear framework for *how* a collaborative culture will:

- Require a common, districtwide vocabulary to articulate shared understanding
- Take team responsibility for the learning progress of all students in every class, course, or grade level
- Collectively and continuously access research on best practices to improve student learning
- Collaboratively collect and analyze data to specifically assess the effectiveness of instructional strategies and, more generally, the overall learning success of students
- Regularly observe the best practice instruction of others

Strategists must also remember their responsibility to model districtwide collaboration. While operationalists need to answer to tacticians, and tacticians need to answer to strategists, strategists need to answer to no one in the district on a day-to-day basis. That is why a strategist's willingness to model collaboration is crucial to having tacticians and operationalists embrace this idea. They can do this by:

- Being open to understanding the impact of strategic charges on tactical and operational responsibilities—the cascading effect
- Being willing to bring tacticians and operationalists into long-range strategic discussions

- Setting timelines with the needs of tacticians and operationalists in mind
- Acting on behalf of the entire district, rather than from the strategic perspective alone

What Kohm and Nance (2009) state about principals is equally true of strategists: "Principals who need to raise achievement are driving with the brakes on unless they build cultural norms that support faculty working together" (p. 67).

Table 4.1: Role Responsibilities for Shared Mission, Vision, Values, and Goals

Strategic	Tactical	Operational
1. Set clear direction for the district through mission, vision, values, and a set of limited and focused long-range strategic goals.	1.1 Articulate, protect, and promote a common mission and vision.	1.1.1 Contribute to the attainment of the district's mission and vision. 1.1.2 Incorporate the district's mission and vision into the work done at the classroom, team, and school levels.
	1.2 Establish and enforce common values and collective commitments that serve to align behaviors and actions to the mission and vision.	1.2.1 Contribute to the development and understanding of common values and collective commitments. 1.2.2 Align behaviors and actions with the district's common values and collective commitments.
	1.3 Establish long-range goals, limit priorities and initiatives, and provide rationales that connect the district's work with the attainment of the district's desired future.	1.3.1 Use the district's goals, indicators, measures, and targets to align improvement efforts at classroom, team, and school levels. 1.3.2 Focus on the priorities and initiatives that connect the organization's work with the attainment of the district's desired future. 1.3.3 Reflect on the rationale to understand how initiatives connect with the attainment of the district's desired future. 1.3.4 Keep the desired future of the district as the aligned goal of the classroom, team, and school.

Tactical Responsibilities

Central office administrators and principals need to be mindful of three broad tactical responsibilities with regard to this non-negotiable: (1) articulating, protecting, and promoting the strategic mission and vision; (2) establishing and enforcing common values and collective commitments; and (3) coordinating initiatives and priorities with the long-range strategic goals.

Articulating, Protecting, and Promoting the Strategic Mission and Vision

This begins with building a common language with which people at different role levels can discuss the same things in the same words that result in the same understandings. We saw how crucial this is in the story about how a focus on learning got derailed in the Nirvana School District (pages 50–51). Key terminology should be identified and consistently used across the district so that discussions about student learning do not have to be translated between grade levels, departments, and schools. Confusion over what key terminology means will slow progress and generate opposition over what should be common beliefs and values.

While the strategic expectation of a common language should be tight, the development of the common definitions that comprise a common language needs to be loose. In this sense, *loose* means that although there is a clear expectation for a common language, its development needs to be the result of a collaborative give and take between and among the tactical and operational roles. Michael Fullan (2002) urges tacticians to recognize that teachers need to "make meaning" of their practice, and an important aspect of that is reaching consensus on the definitions of key terminology. Teachers won't be able to consistently and effectively collaborate unless they embrace a common language, and they are unlikely to do so unless they are a part of the process that determines it.

Establishing and Enforcing Common Values and Collective Commitments

Tacticians set expectations that everyone is expected to meet. At this stage, these expectations focus on the commitments of tactical and operational teams at department and grade levels districtwide. These collective commitments are specific and formally stated.

Principals and other administrators filling the tactical role can actively look for opportunities to promote and celebrate collaborative cultures in schools and make collaboration a centerpiece of their continuous improvement efforts. Because principals know that faculties take note of where principals spend their time, they can also model the importance of a collaborative culture by regularly visiting teams and spending as much time supervising their effectiveness as they do supervising individual teachers in the traditional way.

As tacticians, principals accept responsibility for creating the conditions that support collaborative relationships among teachers, including alterations to the schedule and creating procedures for regularly communicating with teams. In many cases, the look and feel of faculty meetings change as a result. Instead of teachers sitting and listening to the principal dispense information, they attend as teams and solve problems.

Aligning Initiatives and Priorities to Long-Term Strategic Goals

This is a tactical "gatekeeper" responsibility for building high-performing teams. Because there are usually more initiatives than time and resources to carry them out, the tendency is for each role to create its own priorities in isolation from those of other roles. This overwhelms the district with too many individual and uncoordinated priorities. Someone in the district has to make sure role priorities align to strategic goals and work to eliminate those that don't.

Tacticians must also thin out those initiatives that are not contributing to the improvement of learning, and they must do this with the needs of all three roles in mind—no small task. Failing to do so results in lots of confusion and initiatives that don't accomplish what they were designed to accomplish.

Operational Responsibilities

The expectation for creating a collaborative culture represents a major shift for many teachers. The notion that the development of a guaranteed and viable curriculum, design of common assessments, purposeful analysis of data, intentional modification of instruction, continuous pursuit of best practices, provision of more support for students who learn with difficulty, and universally high levels of student learning are *collective* responsibilities transforms the teaching and learning process.

This shift is reflected in two significant operational behavior changes. First, the strategic mission and vision and accompanying common values and collective commitments connect directly to classroom decisions about what and how to teach. This puts all teachers on a team on the same page regarding curriculum and instruction.

Second, the tactical prioritizing and culling of initiatives flow down to team and classroom decisions. Anyone who has ever worked in a school system knows how significant—and difficult—it is for teachers to *stop* doing what may be well established but is not advancing learning.

To expect the members of a collaborative team to assist each other in doing this is challenging but possible; to expect individual teachers to make these kinds of shifts—much less make them all together in some magically aligned fashion—is unrealistic.

Also at an operational level, teachers need to make effective and efficient use of time to improve student performance. They accomplish this by carrying out discussions around student learning results, leading to shared goals regarding student growth and achievement. These discussions and the decisions that evolve from teams depend on having designated and protected time together.

High-Performing Collaborative Teams

The second non-negotiable for a collaborative culture is creating high-performing collaborative teams. This non-negotiable represents what Bossidy, Charan, and Burck (2002) refer to as the "hardware" of teams and involves how teams organize and train themselves—that is, how they create collaborative structures and processes.

Barth (2006) identifies the importance of collaborative teams this way:

> A precondition for doing *anything* to strengthen our practice and improve a school is the existence of a collegial culture in which professionals talk about practice, share their craft knowledge, and observe and root for the success of one another. Without these in place, no meaningful improvement—no staff or curriculum development, no teacher leadership, no student appraisal, no team teaching, no parent involvement, and no sustained change—is possible. (p. 13)

Lencioni (2002) captures the elements of highly effective collaborative teams:

> TRUST—members of great teams trust one another on a fundamental, emotional level, and they are comfortable being vulnerable with each other about their weaknesses, mistakes, fears, and behaviors. They get to a point where they can be completely open with one another, without filters.
>
> COLLABORATION THROUGH DECISION-MAKING—Teams that trust one another are not afraid to engage in passionate dialogue around issues and decisions that are key to the school's success. They do not hesitate to disagree with, challenge, and question one another, all in the spirit of finding the best answers, discovering the truth, and making great decisions.
>
> COMMITMENT THROUGH PROFESSIONAL BEHAVIORS—Teams that engage in unfiltered conflict are able to achieve genuine buy-in around important decisions, even when various members of the team initially disagree. That's because they ensure that all opinions and ideas are put on the table and considered, giving confidence to team members that no stone has been left unturned.
>
> ACCOUNTABILITY THROUGH PROFESSIONAL ACTIONS—Teams that commit to decisions and standards of performance do not hesitate to hold one another accountable for adhering to those decisions and standards. What is more, they don't rely on the team leader as the primary source of accountability; they go directly to their peers.
>
> RESULTS THROUGH GROWTH AND IMPROVEMENT—Teams that trust one another, engage in conflict, commit to decisions, and hold one another accountable are very likely to set aside their individual needs and agendas and focus almost exclusively on what is best for the team. They do not give in to the temptation to place their departments, grade level teams, career aspirations, or ego-driven status ahead of the collective results that define team success. (p. 4)

Table 4.2 illustrates the specific aligned responsibilities each role assumes in creating high-performing collaborative teams.

Table 4.2: Role Responsibilities for High-Performing Collaborative Teams

Strategic	Tactical	Operational
2. Approve and support specific policies, practices, and procedures that foster the development of high-performing collaborative teams.	2.1 Establish team structures and enforce the expectation that all teachers will be members of and meet regularly in collaborative teams by class, course, or grade level.	2.1.1 Provide input into team membership composition. 2.1.2 Implement collaborative team structures and strategies. 2.1.3 Attend frequent, focused, and facilitated collaborative team meetings.
	2.2 Establish team-based roles to enhance the effectiveness and efficiency of collaborative teams.	2.2.1 Provide collaborative input in the development of team roles to enhance the effectiveness of collaborative teams. 2.2.2 Facilitate opportunities to develop and utilize teacher team leaders, including facilitating schoolwide leadership teams. 2.2.3 Provide team leaders the data to share learning successes and needs with other teams.
	2.3 Facilitate the establishment of agreed-upon norms and protocols to guide and assess the behaviors and work of collaborative teams.	2.3.1 Create and utilize specific norms and protocols to enhance the effectiveness of collaborative teams. 2.3.2 Regularly assess and refine the effective use of team norms used to guide the behaviors of the collaborative teams. 2.3.3 Regularly assess and refine the effective use of team protocols used to guide the work of the collaborative teams.
	2.4 Establish and enforce the expectation that individuals work collaboratively with other team members to take responsibility for the learning of every student taught by any member or members of the team.	2.4.1 Assume a collective team responsibility and accountability for the learning progress of each student within the team. 2.4.2 Document and share the team's collective commitment to improving the progress of all students taught by any team members.

continued →

Strategic	Tactical	Operational
2. Approve and support specific policies, practices, and procedures that foster the development of high-performing collaborative teams. *(continued)*	2.5 Establish a professional environment for sharing, comparing, and reporting data so as to enhance learning.	2.5.1 Accept responsibility for results collectively—as a team—rather than individually. 2.5.2 Openly share results within the collaborative team. 2.5.3 Address successful results as a cause for collective team celebration. 2.5.4 Address unsuccessful results as a cause for further exploration and investigation by the team. 2.5.5. Collaboratively plan the next round of instruction based on the results of common assessments of student learning.
	2.6 Establish the expectation that the work of collaborative team time is monitored on a regular basis.	2.6.1 Utilize agreed-upon guidelines, schedules, and deadlines for the efficient management of the teacher team meetings. 2.6.2 Monitor the frequency and quality of the participation of all team members in collaborative team activities. 2.6.3 Reflect on the work of the team, and as an individual member of the team, against high-performing team criteria.
	2.7 Facilitate horizontal and vertical articulation to promote the systematic and systemic implementation of intentionally collaborative practices.	2.7.1 Actively participate in periodic horizontal team meetings within grade levels or departments to ensure systematic implementation. 2.7.2 Actively participate in periodic vertical team meetings across grade levels or departments to ensure systemic implementation.
3. Promote collaborative partnerships among the board of education, district administration, school administrators, the teachers union, other staff unions, parents, and students.	3.1 Facilitate collaborative board, administrative, and teacher union partnerships at the district level.	3.1.1. Support the teachers union in partnership efforts with the board and administration regarding the application of mission, vision, values, and strategic goals in all schools.

Strategic	Tactical	Operational
3. Promote collaborative partnerships among the board of education, district administration, school administrators, the teachers union, other staff unions, parents, and students. *(continued)*	3.2 Align district partnerships to the collaborative work of the schools through common mission, vision, values, and strategic goals.	3.2.1. Align collaborative team efforts and activities to the district's mission, vision, values, and strategic goals.

Strategic Responsibilities

At a strategic level, responsibilities for creating high-performing teams manifest themselves through clear, concise, and consistent policy statements—and, if necessary, by adjustments to the collective bargaining agreement—so that all teachers understand the importance of being regular, contributing members of teams. It also means that administrators collaborate to support the teacher teams. The policy expectation must be clear and explicit: *everyone will participate.*

To support this expectation, strategists need to walk their collaborative talk by promoting partnerships across all roles and constituent groups. Boards of education, school administration, district administration, unions, parents, and students all need to work together to create a collaborative culture throughout every level of the district.

Strategists need to seek out and act on perception data from other roles and constituents, including students. In practical terms, board retreats and strategic visioning events need to have tactical and operational representatives and participants, and a true customer service orientation needs to manifest itself in district actions and initiatives. Ultimately, a collaborative culture is not about who makes which decisions as much as it is about aligning the decisions made by each role with actions taken by the other roles.

Tactical Responsibilities

Tactical responsibilities for high-performing collaborative teams include clear and explicitly stated expectations that teams will take responsibility for every student's learning and for establishing a professional environment that encourages the comparing, sharing, and airing of student achievement data and the use of instructional best practices.

Tacticians must also clear away the impediments to establishing teams. Principals operating at the tactical level establish systematic processes and procedures for ensuring that teams have time to meet and for monitoring how teams use that time, how effectively they are collaborating, and what each team is doing to improve student learning. They check that each team has created norms, developed SMART goals, and adopted agreed-upon criteria for the use of protocols for data analysis. They also determine common expectations for products and artifacts and facilitate observation of teachers by other teachers. Specific tactical responsibilities in this area include:

- Monitoring effectiveness through data-based evidence
- Determining (but not assigning) roles and responsibilities that represent school-wide team expectations
- Facilitating the development of specific norms for each team
- Facilitating the development of specific protocols for each team
- Facilitating horizontal (within grades or departments) and vertical (across grades or departments) articulation among and between teams

It is important to take a moment to delineate the difference between norms and protocols, and to see how each promotes the work of collaborative teams.

A norm consists of general guidelines that address the expected behavior of teams. According to Beatty and Scott (2004), "Norms are those consistent and enduring behaviors that group members have explicitly or implicitly agreed to. They support a set of shared beliefs, values, and expectations for team behavior and determine how we do things around here" (p. 39). Norms are the cultural rules—both written and unwritten—that govern how the members of effective high-performing teams "work and play" with one another.

Protocols are specific guidelines that ensure that the daily conversations among teachers are productive. In effect, they are a team's "rules of the road" for having focused, nonjudgmental debates and conversations. Most protocols consist of a structured format that includes a tentative time frame and specific guidelines for communication among team members. Descriptions of protocols typically identify the purpose, number of participants, time required, roles of team members, and expected outcomes.

Protocols help a team dig deeper and create a safe conversational environment for individuals. Team members who adopt protocols know what to expect. They know they'll hear constructive feedback and will be provided time to offer input into conversations. Protocols expressly call for candid conversations, but those conversations have clearly defined boundaries that delineate the conversation's purposes.

When necessary, principals must be willing to confront individual teachers who behave in ways that are inconsistent with expectations for members of high-performing teams. Through experience, we have come to understand that team effectiveness exists on a continuum—some teams are simply more effective than others. Principals should not expect teams to go from bad—or even good—to great without some help.

Dysfunctional teams ignore behaviors that support high performance. They look away when the norms, values, and practices of a PLC are violated. They engage in the most superficial kinds of collaboration, often publicly agreeing to work that promotes high levels of student learning, only to return to the privacy of their rooms, where they shut the door and continue doing what they have always done. Teachers on these teams still operate on the premise that it is better to "go along to get along" rather than confront their colleagues around unproductive behaviors. Confronting such behaviors is part of a principal's tactical responsibilities.

Good teams ask their principals for help in dealing with the negative behaviors of toxic team members that they are unwilling to tolerate any longer. Great teams have developed and evolved to the point where they are able—through norms and protocols—to handle these kinds of issues themselves.

Operational Responsibilities

At an operational level, teacher teams need to develop and follow guidelines in order to collaborate. This is where the differences between collaborative team planning, which focuses on how to respond to the four critical questions of learning, and individual teacher planning time, which is focused on preparation, are most striking.

Collaborative teams understand that "teacher conversations must quickly move beyond what are we expected to teach to how do we know what each of our students have learned" (DuFour, DuFour, Eaker, & Karhanek, 2004).

Such collaborative conversation is not easy, and disagreements are bound to occur. That is why effectiveness should not be judged merely by ease of discussion. As Fullan, Bertani, and Quinn (2004) write: "Successful districts are collaborative, but they are not always congenial and consensual. Working in a high-trust yet demanding culture, participants view disagreement as a normal part of change and are able to value and work through differences" (p. 45). Collaboration doesn't mean everyone is always happy, but it does mean everyone is committed to solving the same problems, even when they are hard to solve and the solutions are not immediately clear to all.

Creating Intentional Collaboration

The third non-negotiable for a collaborative culture is creating intentional collaboration.

The term *intentional collaboration* is taken directly from Susan Sparks's chapter in *The Collaborative Teacher* (2008), titled "Creating Intentional Collaboration." It represents what Bossidy et al. (2002) refer to as the "software"—or culture—of teams. This non-negotiable focuses on the actual work of a collaborative team and the tools and strategies teams use to attain high levels of learning for students. Intentional collaboration reflects the internal work of collaborative teams. Where the establishment of high-performing teams represented an external commitment *to* the team, intentional collaboration represents an internal commitment *by* the team to such things as norms, protocols, facilitation, and reflection.

Table 4.3 (page 72) illustrates the specific aligned responsibilities each role assumes in creating intentional collaboration.

Table 4.3: Role Responsibilities for Intentional Collaboration

Strategic	Tactical	Operational
4. Approve and support specific policies and expectations that require intentional collaboration.	4.1 Require that the work of collaborative teams reflect an understanding of the four critical questions of learning.	4.1.1 Perform regular and routine analyses of student learning results, and compare them to individual student and team learning goals and targets. 4.1.2 Submit products and artifacts that demonstrate how collaborative activities are addressing the four critical questions.
	4.2 Monitor the effectiveness of instructional choices made by collaborative teams as measured by results.	4.2.1 Engage in collective inquiry about how to continually improve student learning through more focused and improved instructional decisions. 4.2.2 Continually adjust instructional choices based on frequent data collection of results. 4.2.3 Maintain ongoing records, based on common templates used by all teams that document the instructional choices of the collaborative teams and their success in improving student learning.
	4.3 Develop team members' capacity to learn from and with each other.	4.3.1 Engage in structured learning opportunities, such as book studies and literature reviews that promote professional learning. 4.3.2 Observe the instructional best practices of other teachers during the regular school day. 4.3.3 As a result of learning together, continually adjust the team's consensus of how best to address the four critical questions of learning.

Strategic	Tactical	Operational
4. Approve and support specific policies and expectations that require intentional collaboration. *(continued)*	4.4. Monitor to ensure all teams are collaboratively addressing the four critical questions of learning.	4.4.1. Reach consensus on what students should be able to do as a result of their class, course, or grade level. 4.4.2. Measure, through ongoing assessments, the progress of each student in reaching mastery of the essential outcomes for the class, course, or grade level. 4.4.3. Provide schoolwide, systematic pyramids of intervention that give additional time and support aligned to specific student learning needs. 4.4.4. Provide schoolwide, systematic strategies such that students who have demonstrated mastery are provided opportunities to extend and enrich their learning.
	4.5 Monitor the level of intentional collaboration on a team through review of practices, artifacts, and protocols.	4.5.1 Protect collaborative team time so it is only used to address issues that directly affect improving student learning. 4.5.2. Document through artifacts, products, and protocols how instruction has been altered to address the learning needs of particular students. 4.5.3 Maintain ongoing records, based on common templates used by all teams to record the activities of the collaborative team meetings that focus on instructional best practices.

Strategic Responsibilities

At a strategic level, the responsibility for creating intentional collaboration is limited to establishing the expectation that implementation of structures for a collaborative culture must actually take place. However, strategists don't go *beyond* sending that strategic message. For this non-negotiable, the direct actions of strategists are limited to modeling the collaborative practices themselves. This helps strategists credibly justify their collaborative expectations of others.

Tactical Responsibilities

For the previous non-negotiable, principals established systems for monitoring the establishment and structure of teams. In creating intentional collaboration, principals engage in the tactical activities of monitoring the work of teams. This means acquiring first-hand knowledge of what teams are doing.

The documentation principals use to monitor the work of teams flows from the four critical questions (page 29), and the team's products and artifacts become evidence of teams' success in addressing these questions. Effective principals meet regularly with teams to review the implementation of the guaranteed and viable curriculum, reflect on the progress of individual students, and participate in discussions about how to ensure that all students learn.

Richard Elmore (2006) encourages principals to embrace the concept of reciprocal accountability when monitoring team effectiveness (see page 25). Only then can principals know where they need additional support. Some principals adopt specific forms to structure team meetings and agendas. Others require that teams share their meeting minutes or journals on a weekly basis. An increasing number are incorporating technology by using email and podcasts. Whatever method is used, reciprocal accountability requires a continuous flow of information between the principal and the teams.

This flow of information centers around the learning results produced by teams, exemplified by the sharing of results derived from a team's SMART goals. It is only through shared knowledge of each team's impact on improving learning that the principal can accurately determine the true effectiveness of that team. This makes knowledge of a team's structure and routines necessary for helping a principal understand and support team needs, but such knowledge is secondary to that principal's assessment of the team's effectiveness. Effectiveness must ultimately be determined by the learning progress its students.

A comprehensive compilation of a team's learning results gives both the team and the team's supervisor a rich source of documentation by which to assess effectiveness. It allows the supervisor to make results-based judgments on the *team's* effectiveness through objective data. This creates a strong argument that monitoring such data is a more effective use of a principal's supervisory time than are the more traditional and time-consuming individual teacher observations. Monitoring of such continually evolving data can be a powerful supervisory tool, especially given that such monitoring is directly aligned to a focus on learning.

However, simply monitoring progress is not enough. Effective principals model behaviors that promote collaboration. They intentionally change the format of faculty meetings, facilitate difficult conversations among teams, and constantly seek out opportunities to celebrate teachers' collaborative efforts.

One of the tactician's expectations-setting responsibilities is to get agreement on a regular schedule of reporting and documentation. While teams need time and autonomy to perform their collaborative work, they still need to establish common expectations around what that work will be and how it will take place.

An example of one such expectation is developing structures around how team time is to be used. Simply supplying the time and the list of resources to meet doesn't mean teachers will know how to productively use them. Indeed, given their experience of teaching in isolation, it can be safely assumed most will not know how to use team time well without some training and assistance. To that end, tacticians need to supply and require staff development for teachers on how to use and document their time together.

This includes principals helping teams determine what kinds of data to collect and how to analyze such data effectively—how to use a team's SMART goal results and other data-based team tools. Most teachers feel they don't have access to the data they most need, don't know how to draw conclusions from the data they do have, don't conceive of what they already produce as being sources of usable data, or don't know how to take a variety of data and draw conclusions from that data mix. Assisting teachers in how to quickly yet effectively analyze data is as necessary as helping teachers manage those data.

Operational Responsibilities

At an operational level, successful collaborative teams are not only high performing, they also generate artifacts that document their effectiveness. Just as student learning can be documented through data, so can the work of the collaborative teacher team be documented through artifacts. In a collaborative culture, artifacts become one of the key indicators for teacher appraisal: how does the individual teacher add to the overall value and effectiveness of the team?

Artifacts include "lists of essential outcomes, different kinds of assessments, analyses of student achievement, and strategies for improving results" (DuFour et al., 2007). They serve as both evidence of a focus on learning and as exemplars of desired future performance. Artifacts also serve as part of the evidence used to assess the commitment of teachers to student learning required by an aligned teacher appraisal system. And finally, artifacts are a bridge between tactical (principal) monitoring and operational (teacher) actions.

To the extent that principals and teachers discuss and review these artifacts together, each needs to align its efforts with those of the other—principals do so by learning what additional resources can be provided to teachers, and teachers do so by giving specific feedback to the principal regarding what is or is not successful in improving learning.

Teachers demonstrate their professional commitment to intentional collaboration by what they do—and document—as ongoing learners. This means no teacher should remove himself or herself from the collective commitments of the team, including its ongoing learning experiences, such as action research, lesson study, learning circles, and book studies and literature reviews.

Action Research

Action research involves taking best practice strategies and approaches, trying them out in the classroom, collecting data on the results, and comparing them to previous results to see if the new intervention improved student learning. A commitment to action research implies a commitment to eliminating less effective instructional practices in favor of more proven ones, rather than just hanging on to what is most familiar and comfortable.

Lesson Study

One commonly used model for promoting professional learning and improving a teacher's pedagogy is lesson study (Lewis, 2004). Teams of teachers involved in lesson study engage in a cycle of inquiry around a single lesson to refine and sharpen their pedagogy. A typical lesson study cycle lasts three to four months, though some last as long as a year.

According to Lewis (2004), lesson study, which originated in Japan, consists of five steps that teachers take together:

1. Form goals for student learning and long-term development. Teachers study existing curricula and standards and discuss the qualities they would like to have students have five or ten years later.

2. Collaboratively plan a lesson designed to bring to life both immediate and long-term goals.

3. Teach the lesson, with one team member teaching and others gathering evidence on student learning and development.

4. Discuss the evidence they gather during the lesson, using it to improve the lesson, the unit, and overall instruction.

5. Teach the revised lesson in another classroom, if they desire, and study and improve it again. (p. 175)

Through this cycle, teachers not only deepen their content knowledge and sharpen their pedagogy, but they also increase their access to knowledgeable colleagues (Lewis, 2004).

Learning Circles

Learning circles (Riel, 2006) are another way teams can collaboratively sharpen their pedagogy and deepen their content knowledge. Learning circles consist of a six-step process that addresses the collaborative improvement of teaching and learning. The purpose of this or any similar program is not to replace existing curricula but to mine new or more effective approaches to instruction that will increase student learning in a teacher's classroom and within a teacher's collaborative team.

Books Studies and Literature Reviews

In a similar fashion, book studies and literature reviews carried out by the collaborative team expose teachers to emerging best practices, build shared knowledge, and provide further opportunities for action research. Here is one fictional example from the Nirvana School District.

Math Department Literature Review

The seventh-grade math department decided to work on a goal to improve instructional strategies around algebraic equations. They decided to read one article on lesson study and another on learning circles. Then they discussed both articles to decide which model the team should follow to improve its instructional strategies. Down the hall, the science department selected a book on emerging technologies for a team book study. Their discussions of a chapter every two weeks allowed them to build useful background knowledge for the "going green" unit they would be teaching in the spring. And in the primary wing of the school, the third-grade team agreed to discuss one article a month that centered on improving vocabulary development. Each team member would be responsible for selecting one article for the team.

In all three cases, each team decided on its study topic by aligning the topic to one of the team's SMART goals for the year. By aligning the topics to the SMART goals, the teams had a ready bank of data available to inform them of the impacts of their instructional changes around a focus on learning, deepened their content knowledge through the study, sharpened their pedagogy through new ideas and applications, and collaboratively developed a deeper understanding of the entire teaching and learning processes.

In this way, teams can systematically provide powerful, ongoing learning opportunities for themselves.

Alignment Constants

Table 4.4 (pages 78–80) shows the role responsibilities for the four alignment constants—(1) policies, practices, and procedures; (2) monitoring and reporting; (3) resources and training; and (4) an aligned appraisal system—as they apply to building and sustaining a collaborative culture.

Strategic Responsibilities

At a strategic level, a resources and training application that supports a collaborative culture is the requirement that teams of teachers meet on a regular and ongoing basis during the normal school day. Ideally, this is as often as the teams deem necessary to effectively manage all of the work expected of them, but teams certainly should not meet less than weekly. This commitment will likely cost the district additional money, but we would argue there is no better value for the dollars spent if the desired result is a high-performing collaborative culture.

Table 4.4: Role Responsibilities for the Alignment Constants for Building a Collaborative Culture

Alignment Constant	Strategic	Tactical	Operational
Policies, practices, and procedures	5. Require an analysis, by school and district office, of the policies, practices, and procedures that do and do not align with a collaborative culture, followed by an action plan for addressing those policies, practices, and procedures that are not aligned.	5.1 Produce a summary, by school and district office, of practices and procedures that do not align with a collaborative culture, and create specific recommendations as to what can be done to better align to that end.	5.1.1 Review policies, practices, and procedures that align with a collaborative culture. 5.1.2 Celebrate those policies, practices, and procedures that are in alignment, and act on what needs to be changed in those that remain unaligned.
		5.2 Provide examples of best practices, through literature and experiences, for stakeholders to communicate compelling rationales for making shifts from where we are to where we need to be around a collaborative culture.	5.2.1 Ensure that teaching practices are in line with best practice research aligned to a collaborative culture. 5.2.2 Examine present practices and procedures by experimenting with doing things differently to get better results.
Aligned appraisal systems	6. Require district appraisal systems to align the non-negotiables for a collaborative culture with the standards for performance.	6.1 Ensure that the non-negotiables for a collaborative culture are aligned to the performance appraisal feedback systems.	6.1.1 Collect appraisal assessment data, aligned to the non-negotiables for a collaborative culture, through self, peer/team, and supervisor assessment data. 6.1.2 Use appraisal assessment data to establish professional growth plans and actions that lead to improved student and teacher performance.

Alignment Constant	Strategic	Tactical	Operational
Aligned appraisal systems *(continued)*		6.2 Use non-negotiables for a collaborative culture to guide recruitment, selection, induction, retention, mentoring, and professional growth.	6.2.1 Provide input into the recruitment and selection of new staff against the non-negotiables for a collaborative culture. 6.2.2 Mentor others to develop capacity to deploy and sustain the non-negotiables for a collaborative culture.
Resources and training	7. Align resources for support and training to ensure systematic and systemic deployment of the non-negotiables for a collaborative culture.	7.1 Provide opportunities to learn, apply, and reflect on best practices aligned to the non-negotiables for a collaborative culture.	7.1.1 Participate in professional development to reflect on practice and gain additional tools, skills, strategies, and knowledge to meet district expectations for collaborative culture non-negotiables. 7.1.2 Assist colleagues in meeting district expectations for collaborative culture non-negotiables.
		7.2 Promote an ongoing expectation that a continual study and sharing of best practices, aligned to a collaborative culture, will be modeled by administrators and expected of teachers.	7.2.1 Participate as an active, contributing member of a team that commits to regular and continual study and sharing of instructional and learning best practices to ensure a collaborative culture. 7.2.2 Identify changes in practices that link to measurably improved results.

continued →

Alignment Constant	Strategic	Tactical	Operational
Monitoring and reporting	8. Require at each level of the system—student, classroom, team/department, school, program, and district—that improvement efforts, through deployment of non-negotiables for a collaborative culture, be monitored and reported.	8.1 Monitor system requirements through agenda planning and focused discussion to assess progress related to collaborative culture non-negotiables.	8.1.1 Examine teaching and learning results to see if improvements are being made based on collaborative culture non-negotiables. 8.1.2 Share strategies to further guide improvement or redirect improvement efforts. 8.1.3 Track progress through data charts, graphs, or logs.

A districtwide commitment to dedicated and protected team meeting time is also critical to establishing credibility with teachers regarding their commitment to intentional collaboration. When strategists or tacticians state that something is a goal, they need to make it a goal for operationalists as well, but they can do this only by placing the goal in its proper operational context. Making designated and protected time for teams to meet during the regular school day a priority gives credibility to the goal of establishing high-performing collaborative teams. Stating that collaborative team time is a priority but not giving teachers time during the regular day to meet will strike teachers as disingenuous at best, as DuFour et al. (2010) note when they state, "We believe it is insincere for any district or school leader to stress the importance of collaboration and then fail to provide time for it" (p. 124). This is a textbook example of refusing to accept the obligations that come with reciprocal accountability (Elmore, 2006).

Another strategic priority, the requirement for standard products and artifacts from teacher teams, is also based on the strategist's commitment to providing the resources—in this instance, time—for those teacher teams to hold meetings that are productive and advance the development of a tight focus on student and adult learning.

Strategists have a right to expect that this time will be used appropriately—another practical example of reciprocal accountability. This expectation—that team time is focused on improving student learning—is tight, but the conclusions teachers will arrive at as a result of their collaborative time spent remain loose.

Tactical Responsibilities

A tactical example of an alignment constant is aligning the expectations of teams to the teacher appraisal system. Collaboration is more likely to be sustained if teacher performance reviews focus on the work and responsibilities of teams, not just individuals. At the very least, the reviews should include a section on expectations of and contributions to the team as part of an individual teacher's appraisal. To do otherwise sends competing messages to staff about which is more important—team expectations or the individual's performance appraisal criteria.

A tactical example of the resources and training constant is a master schedule that intentionally establishes designated and protected planning time during the regular school day. In practice, the costs and complexities of scheduling often override the logic behind the goal of common team planning time. Creating a master schedule that places a priority on planning time usually means embracing some challenging new assumptions.

In schools where teaching is the driving assumption behind the master schedule, it is not uncommon for the needs of elementary specials teachers (art, music, and physical education) to dictate the master schedule. A typical schedule might show all first-grade specials classes scheduled one after another. This approach makes sense if the goal of the master schedule is to facilitate the art or physical education teacher's management of equipment, materials, or supplies.

However, while transitions between grade levels are minimized, opportunities to release teachers from the same grade level simultaneously for planning are also minimized. In these schools, facilitating the logistics of a specials teacher's day becomes the primary concern, making generating common planning time for teams a secondary concern.

As an alternative, consider a specials schedule where creating common planning time for teacher teams is the number-one priority. In these schools, the principal identifies blocks of time when all of the first-grade classes have art, music, physical education, computer lab, or any number of other special offerings, all during the same part of the day.

During the time students are assigned to one of the available specials classes, teachers from that grade level are free to meet as teams. These teachers use this common planning time to clarify what students should know and be able to do, design common assessments, and work through the logistics of systematic pyramids of intervention for students who need it.

Schedules are occasionally flexed for any number of reasons, from schoolwide projects to field trips to assemblies to special integrated unit experiences. Will collaborative team time be sacrificed to accommodate these additional activities, or will team time remain a scheduled priority? In a school culture committed to collaboration, team time always takes first priority.

Operational Responsibilities

An operational example of the resources and training constant is when collaborative teams make teacher training recommendations based not just on what is interesting to some teachers but also on what could help collaborative teams address the four critical questions more effectively.

This represents a focused use of operational expertise. When all district roles are aligned for the same purpose, role expertise becomes more relevant. And when this role expertise is directed toward identifying training needs that will make the team more effective, it greatly increases the benefits of the training.

Of course, a team's recommendations for training are only half the equation. Those recommendations need to then be heard and acted on by tacticians. This requires a more nimble staff development model—much closer to a mentor approach—than most districts typically provide. Within this approach, ongoing teacher training is predominantly delivered at the collaborative team level, rather than the school or district levels, since that is where the training will have the most direct classroom impact.

This also requires training that is differentiated by team. Even though they will have time to share practices and learn from one another, teams also need outside training opportunities and resources tailored specifically to each team's unique needs, not just to generic school needs.

This also raises the question of how principals can most effectively support teachers. A case can be made that if training should be differentiated by team, supervision should be differentiated by team as well. If the collaborative teacher team is the fundamental building block of a professional learning community, doesn't it make sense for principals to focus their time and energy on supervising teachers as they work together in teams rather than as individuals teaching an isolated lesson?

Supporting teams with differentiated training and supervision is another instance where the roles need to align—strategists to provide resources for training, tacticians to utilize those resources to provide the training opportunities, and operationalists to bring their operational expertise to bear—so the right training is selected.

Case Study for Building a Collaborative Culture

The Nirvana School District story that follows illustrates how a strategic commitment to collaboration ended up causing major conflicts among strategic, tactical, and operational players. This commitment to collaboration should have been the start of a healthy and successful collaborative effort among the three roles. Instead, the establishment of a collaborative culture was set back significantly, since there was no aligned approach defining how such collaboration should occur.

Do As I Say, Not As I Do

With great anticipation, Superintendent Sue Stanfield prepared for a presentation to her board on the importance of collaboration. She carefully presented the research and shared a painstakingly crafted and well thought-out rationale in support of moving teachers away from working in isolation and toward working in collaborative teams. In her mind, Sue was simply introducing the concept of collaboration to the board of education, thereby setting the stage for a longer and more tactical implementation conversation with members of the faculty and staff.

The presentation was effective, and after hearing the research on the importance of collaboration as manifested in the three big ideas of a professional learning community, the board wanted to ensure that teachers were given every opportunity to collaborate. After a lively discussion, the board passed a resolution requiring that every teacher be a member of a collaborative team. High fives and congratulations were exchanged as the meeting moved on to the list of monthly bills.

The next morning, Sue contacted Nirvana's principals and informed them of the board's action. The east side's high school principal, Howard Blake, who had no training or background in professional learning communities and was in his final year before retirement, asked Sue to "tell him how she wanted the teams organized." Howard honestly did not know or have time to figure out how the teams were to be organized—his priority was trying to fill a coaching vacancy for the boys' varsity basketball team. As one can imagine, weeks passed without anything changing at the building level.

At the next meeting, board president Fran Ackers asked for a status report on the collaborative teams initiative. Sue honestly reported the current east side high school reality and explained that nothing had been done to create the structure, schedule, or membership of teams. No training had been organized. In fact, teachers had not even been told of the board's new decision requiring everyone be a member of a collaborative team. The board's reaction was predictable.

From the board's view, this simple change should already have been put into place. From their perspective, it was an easy fix. Stanley Preston, the president and CEO of a chain of local mortuaries, suggested a memo would suffice. Margaret Richards, a stay-at-home mom, suggested that teachers should be given an opportunity to volunteer for teams of their own choosing, but if they balked at the idea, they should be "volun-told" and simply assigned a collaborative team.

The momentum for immediate, almost instantaneous change took over the meeting. Sue asked for one more month to make the changes. The board, after much wrangling back and forth, eventually agreed, but President Ackers set the creation of teams as a priority item for discussion and/or action on the agenda of the next board committee of the whole meeting.

During the next few weeks Sue met twice with Howard, the teachers association's school representative Nancy Spraggs, the association president Barbara King, and Fran. Howard continued to argue that he did not know how to organize the teams given the existing schedule, Nancy and Barbara resisted any changes that were not a part of the contract, and Fran continued to insist that teams be formed by the end of the month, or else!

By the time the next board meeting took place, the level of frustration had risen to an explosive peak. The original reason why teachers should be organized into collaborative teams had been lost as the board, administration, and teachers' union struggled for power.

Fran Ackers gaveled the board meeting to order and immediately adjourned into closed session with the board's attorney, Malcolm Edwards. During the closed session, attorney Edwards confirmed that legally the board had the "right of assignment" and thus could assign teachers to teams. Given the lack of constructive dialogue between the strategic, tactical, and operational levels of the district, no one had any idea how to organize the teams. The board ultimately mandated that teachers would serve on teams based on how close their teaching stations were. The board reasoned that there would be few logistical issues to resolve by organizing teachers by physical proximity, and teams could begin meeting immediately.

The next day, teachers were scheduled to attend a day-long institute on creating a collaborative culture. The teachers were assigned to sit with their teams—per the board's decision—in an arrangement that reflected the location of their classrooms in the school building. The workshop was a disaster, teachers were outraged at being assigned seats as if they were children, the teaming initiative was abandoned, and everyone blamed everyone else for the fiasco. The last thing on anyone's mind now was collaboration.

Deconstructing the Story: What Went Right

Believe it or not, some things were actually done correctly in this story, although certainly there were fatal errors made.

Strategic

- A presentation to the board on collaboration is helpful and constructive . . . *if* the timing is right and *if* there is an implementation plan to go with the presentation.

- Presenting the research and a strong rationale are two-thirds of what was necessary to make this pitch to the board successful. But a plan to support the research and rationale was missing.

- The initial board reaction—to support collaboration—was the hoped-for outcome of the presentation.

- The board's decision to mandate collaboration—ironic as it may sound—wasn't a bad thing, especially when collaborative teams were considered to be a tight requirement for implementing a successful collaborative culture around a focus on learning. In this case, however, the type and timing of the decision—not the decision itself—are what caused the problem.

Tactical

- The superintendent was correct in realizing that the actual plan for implementing a collaborative culture would require tactical conversations with the principal, faculty, and staff.

- Tying the importance of collaboration to the three big ideas of a PLC represents a sound strategy. Collaboration is part of a bigger picture and that bigger picture should be presented to give the collaborative push its proper context.

- The board had every right to ask for a status report at its next meeting, given that it passed a motion on the topic at its previous meeting and had delegated planning to the superintendent.

- The superintendent *should* have been holding meetings with the three leadership groups—board, principal, and teachers' union—especially because this had become an issue that directly affected all three groups. (But this action is at best a tardy response.)

- A day-long institute to train teachers on the reasons for collaboration is an early step in properly implementing such an initiative—given the proper tactical and operational preparation, which unfortunately did not occur in this instance.

Operational

- Nothing went right operationally. Teachers reacted from a defensive posture due to strategic and tactical decisions that were a surprise to them. The teachers were not angry because they were against collaborating. They were angry because collaboration was being dictated to them.

Admittedly, a number of the choices cited above could only be called "right" under very different circumstances than those reflected in the story. After the initial poor decisions, there were not many constructive options left, no matter what the subsequent decisions.

Deconstructing the Story: What Went Wrong

Here are specific role-based examples from the story of poor actions or flawed decisions.

Strategic

- The superintendent made a grave error in simply introducing the concept of collaboration to the board without also presenting an implementation plan to go with it. At best, she excited the board but gave it nowhere to go. At worst, the board was left to invent somewhere to go itself, which is exactly what happened.

- As soon as the board started thinking it was easy to form teacher teams, it was abandoning its strategic role for a tactical role, where it didn't belong. This was the moment the board's fatal micromanagement first took shape.

- The problem with the board's sequestering itself with its attorney was that this was a political issue—not a legal one. The wrong expert was giving the wrong advice for the situation at hand.

- The board's assumption that teams could begin meeting immediately accounted only for the board's view of the situation. It still had no inkling of the tactical and operational issues, much less how to resolve them.

- Because of the board's overreach, the last thing on anyone's mind was collaboration. If collaboration cannot even be modeled in its earliest stages of development, how could it ever be successfully implemented districtwide?

Tactical

- Because the east side high school principal hadn't even thought about schedules or how to organize the teams, the likelihood of successful implementation at the high school was severely compromised.

- Why wasn't the superintendent more aware of the preretirement status of the principal and how this might affect implementation? Why was she expecting a building leader with no PLC background and no long-term commitment to the school to lead an initiative like this? And if she felt implementation should occur the following year with a new principal, why wasn't that a part of her presentation?

- It was unacceptable for the superintendent to let weeks pass after the board's action with nothing at all changing at the high school. At the very least, the problems in implementation could have been shared with the board, along with a plan and timeline as to how to address them.

- Not telling even the high school teachers about the board action was a crucial communications lapse by the principal and a significant failure to communicate by the superintendent.

- The board's reaction in its second meeting was predictable; the superintendent was completely remiss in not having something to report.

- The request by the superintendent for an extra month was clearly a desperate move. The superintendent now had three intransigent people with whom to try to craft a common agreement.

- The reason teachers should be organized into collaborative teams was completely cast aside as members of each of the three roles positioned themselves to do battle with members of the other two. All felt as if their needs had been ignored, and the collaborative initiative was now the scapegoat for those feelings.

- It is no wonder the workshop was a disaster, since the workshop on collaboration came about through a complete lack of collaboration in its planning and presentation!

Operational

- Clearly, teachers were defensive from the outset. But in fairness to them, they reacted as anyone else would react whose day-to-day activities were fundamentally changed without notice or input. It is hard to embrace collaboration when one is not allowed to say anything about it.

How could have this fiasco been avoided? Here is how this story could have turned out had implementation been carried out collaboratively, role by role.

Revisiting the Story

At a strategic level, Superintendent Sue Stanfield spoke to district principals and teacher union leadership long before any presentation before the board took place. She stressed the purpose for wanting collaborative teams and then elicited tactical and operational concerns connected to establishing collaborative teams so those concerns could be planned for before anything went before the board.

Sue, working with board president Fran Ackers and teachers association president Barbara King, then asked the board to support an implementation plan based on her recommendation. The plan showed clear tactical and operational involvement and support, modeled by principal and teacher representatives who were part of the presentation before the board. They identified tactical and operational concerns and explained possible solutions. The board then endorsed the plan in a decision that appeared to staff as supportive rather than intrusive.

Sue made sure the plan would address the pending retirement of east side high school principal Howard Blake. Any number of solutions might have worked: helping Howard with scheduling, delaying implementation, enlisting Assistant Principal Kerri Hickok's help to assume the responsibility for this initiative, and so on. All of these options represent the "how" of an implementation plan. "How" decisions

continued →

are particularly conducive to collaboration and have a much better chance of garnering support from all roles. The "what"—having collaborative teams—remains the same for each option and rightfully remains a tight non-negotiable.

Sue had also considered whether the board would prefer knowing about her plan in advance, before resources were spent to develop it fully. She had worked this way with another board, presenting only her research and rationale, while noting the need for an implementation plan that would address specific tactical and operational concerns. In the end, she judged that it would be fine to bring the fully developed plan to the current board.

Her plan addressed two big tactical issues: (1) the refusal of Howard to embrace this initiative in his last year before retirement and (2) the need to identify scheduling options and team membership at tactical and operational staff levels, rather than at the board's strategic level.

Handling Howard's lack of commitment to the collaboration initiative was up to Sue, who had three choices: (1) replace him, (2) work with him, or (3) delay implementation. But the true focus here was not about Howard. It was about implementing collaborative teacher teams. The principal issue was only a means to a larger end, not the end itself. If the collaborative teams initiative became a scapegoat among staff because it led to Howard's "martyrdom" through firing, the real issue would be set back rather than promoted.

The other big issues to address were the scheduling changes required and the membership of teacher teams. So which issue trumps the other in importance? The answer: team membership. The team members must be the staff most in contact with the students whose learning is being addressed. Properly addressing scheduling issues required the right teachers teamed together to best maximize student learning. This may make scheduling more difficult to overcome, but so be it. The point wasn't to put teams together to fit the schedule. It was to put a schedule together to fit the meeting needs of the proper teams.

The initial training, well before the final tactical and operational decisions were made, linked the purpose of collaborative teams to the needs of teachers to better assist students in their learning. This approach acknowledged that establishing true collaborative teams represented a major cultural shift, but it also got teachers excited—or at least curious—about the possibilities before they were required to make any changes. It is difficult to both excite people and make major changes at the same time; usually the latter must follow the former—and some training must fall in between. This is a reality that strategists and tacticians often forget, Sue thought.

The institute day was not a disaster. Teachers explored which team members would make the most effective teams. In this way, a team membership resolution came up from the operationalists rather than down from the strategists, automatically creating teacher buy-in and neutralizing the need for teacher union involvement.

Doesn't it seem reasonable to collaborate on a collaboration initiative? mused Sue proudly, as she thought back on the institute day and the progress that was made.

Summary

The story in this chapter represented a full-fledged implementation disaster, and nothing about it had anything to do with the worthiness of establishing collaborative teams. Yet failures to understand the impact of differing roles on a chosen implementation approach doomed the effort. The successful implementation of a collaborative culture was seriously, if not fatally, compromised. A disaster like this is far more difficult to fix than it is to prevent.

Conclusion

This chapter dove into the responsibilities aligned to a collaborative culture and looked at the roles associated with the three non-negotiables for this big idea: (1) shared mission, vision, values, and goals; (2) high-performing collaborative teams; and (3) intentional collaboration. We then examined how the four alignment constants apply to this big idea.

We presented and then deconstructed Nirvana School District's disastrous attempt to impose collaboration from above by unfortunately using a decidedly noncollaborative approach. Then we retold this story, this time as a collaboratively planned and executed effort.

The next chapter focuses on the non-negotiable responsibilities for the third of the three big ideas: a results orientation. We discuss the role-based responsibilities for this idea, and, as before, use a Nirvana story to illustrate the need for an aligned approach in establishing a districtwide results orientation.

chapter five

Aligning to a Results Orientation

Unless a capacity for thinking be accompanied by a capacity for action, a superior mind exists in torture.

—Benedetto Croce

A results orientation isn't about assessing, measuring, and collecting data. It is about *action*. Guskey (2009) makes the case for action this way:

> Measuring something more often and more accurately does nothing to make it better. If that were the case, all that would be required in a successful weight-loss program would be a better scale. Just as being weighed more often and more accurately does not help a person lose weight, the use of regular formative assessment alone does not improve student learning. It's what happens after the formative assessment that makes a difference. (pp. 10–11)

Without a results orientation, the collection of data has no purpose beyond its own collection. With a results orientation, those data convert to new knowledge that drives active changes in instructional approaches and learning expectations.

Let's look at the basic tasks of the three roles for establishing a results orientation.

The Strategic Role

Strategic responsibilities start by establishing parameters for districtwide non-negotiables that define the expectations for a results orientation. For example, strategists would set the parameter "each target needs to exceed previous results." This parameter would describe a tight, districtwide non-negotiable, but strategists would go no further in assigning measures or targets. Strategists need to ensure that the system continuously improves.

Strategists, therefore, also have a responsibility to monitor results. This monitoring responsibility uses results not to micromanage tactics and operations, but to determine whether strategic goals set for the school or district are being met. If targets are not met, strategists then hold tacticians accountable for crafting or altering plans that will meet the targets.

It is important to note that strategic monitoring should not result in punishing tacticians when a viable and research-based intervention doesn't work. Instead, monitoring should result in requiring that another viable and research-based intervention be applied so that an unsuccessful status quo doesn't simply continue as is. It is the *result*— not the person—that should be a strategist's monitoring focus.

A danger for strategists is becoming overly impatient with the pace of school-system change. This often results in strategists setting unrealistic targets or imposing interference in areas of tactical and operational expertise. If student scores aren't where they are supposed to be, something has to be done, and it has to be done *now*! To an impatient strategist, "now" means taking some kind of unilateral action, whether or not it aligns with decisions to which the district is already committed.

Requiring schools that have scored at the state average for years to score within the state's top 10 percent within a year or two; setting a high districtwide target and expecting *all* of the district's schools to hit that same target; imposing a strategic goal to increase the number of students in the gifted program even as certain subgroups of students are failing to meet minimal achievement standards; or dictating the selection of a particular curricular program because some board members have read that this program represents "the miracle cure for academic malaise"—all represent a dangerous strategic impatience, expressed by setting unattainable targets or by assuming responsibilities better left to others.

In each of these examples, the notion of gradual but consistent improvement is strategically abandoned for an attempt at a gallant, if futile, leap to the top. However, since strategists don't teach, all they can do is demand that this great leap occur. This is a clear signal that the strategists' reaction is unrealistic and out of district alignment. When this happens, strategists' demands actually work against rather than toward their desired results.

The Tactical Role

Tactical responsibilities center on crafting and enforcing plans and timelines that bridge strategic impatience for quick change and operational reluctance to embark upon change. Tacticians must tie plans and timelines to measurable outcomes that demonstrate that effective change took place. This is what DuFour et al. (2010) mean when they write that "a critical step in moving an organization from rhetoric to reality is to establish the indicators of progress to be monitored, the process for monitoring them, and the means of sharing results with people throughout the organization" (p. 27).

This requires that tacticians assume responsibility for implementing, monitoring, and enforcing strategic non-negotiables, and setting expectations for how operationalists will implement them in classrooms. This also requires determining districtwide expectations for data efficacy and transparency. Tacticians must, for example, enforce a requirement for common use of a balanced and coherent system of assessment that will produce such data.

The Operational Role

Once formative and summative results have been collected and analyzed, operationalists need to take action by converting these data to new approaches toward how students can improve their learning. Operationally, only when changes in classroom practice take place does a true results orientation exist.

This leads to a functional definition of operational accountability (a definition to which strategists and tacticians should pay particular attention). Accountability is not (a) if the results show all students didn't learn, then (b) some teacher has to be blamed. Accountability shouldn't mean the system automatically seeks a scapegoat when achievement results don't meet targets. Rather, accountability is (a) if the results show all students didn't learn, then (b) how will the team provide those students with more time and support until they do? This definition contributes to the right kind of data culture because it becomes the team's responsibility to ensure the success of all individuals—students and team members—directly affected by the team.

Non-Negotiables for Establishing a Results Orientation

There are three non-negotiables for a results orientation—(1) establishing a data mindset; (2) data management, collection, and analysis; and (3) data-based action to improve results.

Establishing a Data Mindset

The term *data mindset* is derived from the thinking of Douglas Reeves (2008). Establishing a data mindset means collaborative teams and other district levels will regularly use results to assess student learning in a predictable fashion. To paraphrase an observation by Dennis Sparks (2007), it is difficult to establish something when there is no clear picture as to what it should be.

A data mindset also means data as results become far more of a necessity than an optional activity at all district levels. A data mindset welcomes data as formatively diagnostic assets rather than summatively punitive liabilities. To be effective, such a mindset must be embraced consistently at all district levels. Schmoker (1999) describes the characteristics of a sound attitude toward the use of data:

Data can help us confront what we may wish to avoid and what is difficult to perceive, trace or gauge: data can substantiate theories, inform decisions, impel action, marshal support, thwart misperceptions and unwarranted optimism, maintain focus and goal orientation, and capture and sustain collective energy and momentum. (p. 49)

Such an attitude requires a shared commitment to high levels of data efficacy and transparency.

Data efficacy requires the ability to seamlessly collect and compare quality data generated at all levels of the school system. This means data align no matter where they come from or which other data they compare to. The quality criteria for such data are validity—both statistically and in connection to what is actually being taught—and reliability.

Data transparency means data will be used appropriately but shared extensively among appropriate roles. This is an application of Fullan's (2008) contention that "transparency can be abused, such as when results are used punitively, but there is no way that continuous improvement can occur without constant transparency fueled by good data" (p. 14).

This combination of data efficacy and transparency fosters collaborative behaviors around data. At the operational level, teams increase their incentive to collaborate when they have common indicators and are collectively responsible for the same results. At the tactical level, administrators have incentives to support and assist each other when they are all responsible for addressing the same indicators. At the strategic level, the members of the board of education, when focused on districtwide results as their first priority, have a greater incentive to cooperate with each other because effective strategic monitoring, done correctly, will take the majority of their limited time. And all three roles have increased reason to collaborate with each other when common data is driving each of their efforts. The establishment of a data mindset can have a powerfully positive influence on districtwide collaboration, as Henry Louis Gates Jr. testified to when he observed, "Collecting data is only the first step toward wisdom, but sharing data is the first step toward community" (IBM, 2003).

Table 5.1 illustrates the aligned responsibilities each role assumes in establishing a data mindset.

Strategic Responsibilities

Establishing a data mindset is the strategist's most critical responsibility. A districtwide data mindset gives clarity to everyone inside and outside the district regarding promotion of districtwide improvement efforts.

Once a districtwide data mindset is achieved, all three roles adopt an aligned results focus, from the classroom to the boardroom. Outside the district, the consistent reporting of aligned data helps realistically define public expectations and impressions of the district.

Table 5.1: Role Responsibilities for Establishing a Data Mindset

Strategic	Tactical	Operational
1. Approve an aligned, transparent data system—from the classroom to the boardroom—by measuring if students are learning, subgroup performance is equitable, students are connected and engaged, teachers and staff are productive, parents and community are satisfied and supportive, and resources are used effectively and efficiently.	1.1 Recommend essential data sources (indicators of success) that provide evidence of successful attainment for each of the district's long-range goals.	1.1.1 Provide feedback on classroom implications of indicators of success that provide evidence of successful attainment for each of the district's long-range goals. 1.1.2 Demonstrate an understanding of the connected relationship of the indicators of success from the classroom to the board of education.
	1.2 Align appropriate district indicators of success to formative and summative assessments linked to student, classroom, team, and school dashboards or portfolios.	1.2.1 Know how student, classroom, team, and school dashboard data compare with expectations. 1.2.2 Know how student, classroom, team, and school dashboard data compare with other similar data. 1.2.3 Know if student, classroom, team, and school dashboard data are improving over time.
2. Sustain an effective and efficient data-rich culture that encourages and supports continuous improvement.	2.1 Require an effective and efficient data-rich culture that encourages and supports continuous improvement through shared responsibility and accountability.	2.1.1 Ensure effectiveness and efficiency in viewing, monitoring, and reporting student, classroom, team, and school progress through the use of data on a regular basis. 2.1.2 Demonstrate a commitment to shared responsibility for everyone's success.
	2.2 Model and expect shared accountability and ownership of team, school, and districtwide results.	2.2.1 Recognize and celebrate team, school, and districtwide accomplishments. 2.2.2 Focus on team, school, and districtwide opportunities for improvement.

If continuous improvement is to be embraced at tactical and operational levels, strategists—particularly boards of education—must be encouraging rather than discouraging when they publicly report results. Some strategists feel the only way to convince the public they are serious about improving is to highlight the data around failure and, in the name of "accountability," publicly call out a particular school or district staff. Though this grandstanding may please some district critics in the audience, its more far-reaching effect is to make everyone within the district reluctant to share data.

Strategists must therefore be willing to conduct "autopsies without blame" (Reeves, 2010a, p. 11). The kind of data-enriched culture we advocate is hungry for data about its schools, even if it is bad news. If a school or district culture becomes afraid of how individuals will be singled out once data are publicly shared, strategists will deliver a mortal blow to the use of data for continuous improvement.

This is not an argument for reporting only successful data. It is an argument for reporting both successes and failures as either celebrations or opportunities for improvement but not producing scapegoats in the process.

However, a strategic need to model careful public responses to data must nonetheless be balanced by an ongoing drive to move the district forward based on sound evidence for improvement. This calls for strategists to strike a balance between firmness in continually pushing the district toward excellence and sensitivity to those who have to make that excellence happen, day by day, in every classroom and school.

Here we pause to note the difference between strategic monitoring and evaluating. Strategists focus on whether or not the *district* is making progress toward the agreed-upon goals. Evaluation is about identifying how *people* are progressing toward those goals— much more a tactical than a strategic responsibility.

This makes the strategist's role more monitor-based than evaluation-based—the opposite of what one might intuitively conclude. It is well within the board's strategic role to monitor the results of district improvement efforts, but with the exception of evaluating the superintendent, it is not within the board's strategic role to evaluate district employees.

When done properly, this approach toward strategically monitoring progress ensures the process is proactive rather than reactive. When targets are preset and measures align to those targets, strategists don't have to publicly react to the data in a contextual vacuum. This greatly diminishes a strategist's tendency to substitute evaluating for monitoring when responding to disappointing data.

Tactical Responsibilities

Three tactical responsibilities are key to establishing a data mindset—determine scorecard performance indicators, implement the monitoring of the assessment system, and model a shared accountability for results.

The first is to determine performance indicators for school and district scorecards (for a review of scorecards and dashboards, see chapter 2, pages 20–23) tied to formative and summative results. An *indicator* is a statement of the expected level of learning that will be assessed and reported.

The district performance scorecard ties everyone to the same big-picture data. The indicators reflect the alignment to school scorecards and department and grade-level dashboards to follow. Certain indicators—for example, summative results from state achievement and nationally norm-referenced tests or locally developed benchmark assessments—become common to all scorecards and dashboards.

Tacticians also need to monitor the assessment system. At a district level, they need to look at indicators from the district performance scorecard and collect and compare data to see if the data match the indicator statement. This is not a mere statistical exercise. It is a very practical effort to see if what is being measured accurately describes what is being taught. A common mistake is to allow the scorecard's performance indicators to drive their own realities, even when measures from those indicators don't accurately represent what the scorecard purports to measure. If tacticians do not guard against this kind of misrepresentation of data, it is very unlikely anyone else will.

A common example of such an error is when a board of education or the public begins to criticize teacher or administrative performance based only on state test scores. While the results may be disappointing, what is being tested may not accurately represent what is being taught. It is up to administrators to anticipate such criticism, identify where testing and instruction are and are not aligned, and recommend how to close any gaps that exist, thereby providing an accurate context for reacting to the state results. If tacticians don't provide that accurate context, it will likely never become part of the ensuing public discussion.

The final tactical responsibility is to model the principle that accountability for results is shared by everyone. Teachers will balk at the idea of embracing a data mindset if they feel they are the only ones being held accountable for results. This means the entire district, from the board and superintendent on down, needs to join teachers in assuming responsibility for student learning.

Administrative goals and appraisal processes therefore need to be as dependent on results as any teacher's appraisal. Just as teachers are responsible for individual student results and teams are responsible for student group results, principals should be responsible for school results, and central office administration and the board should be responsible for district results. In this way, the levels are aligned by virtue of all having a stake in the success of each student.

Operational Responsibilities

At an operational level, teachers need to see a direct connection between what they do in classrooms and what the district is trying to accomplish. Once again, the district performance scorecard and its approach toward data can assist in this process.

If everyone in each role is focused on the same indicators, each will begin, through the data, to connect his or her own work to the work of others (figs. 5.1–5.3, pages 99–102). One of the achievement indicators in all three figures is ACT 11 math.

In figure 5.1 (pages 99–100), a district performance scorecard shows an ACT math target of 80, a baseline of 76, and a current measure of 80. At a district level, across multiple high schools in the district, the eleventh-grade ACT target overall has been met. In figure 5.2 (page 101), one high school performance scorecard shows the same target of 80, but this high school's current measure falls well short at 70, below even the school's baseline of 74. In this high school, learning as measured by ACT math in eleventh grade has regressed from the previous measure. And in figure 5.3 (page 102), representing one eleventh-grade math department score with the same target, the current measure is 78—an improvement over the baseline of 74 but still short of the target.

At each role level—district, school, and department—the indicator (ACT 11 math) is the same as is, in this case, the target. However, it is the common indicator that links the actions of the district, school, and department together, and this would still be the case even if the targets were not the same.

Because the ACT is a common scorecard or dashboard indicator at each reporting level, it is, by definition, a key indicator of math progress in eleventh grade. So along with other math indicators, the ACT indicator will drive the analysis of the effectiveness of math instruction and curriculum choices. But this analysis must start at the department level, because the only reason learning measures improve is because of classroom—not school or district—instructional and curricular choices. When the department identifies what it will change to meet the target of 80, the subsequent department score will affect the high school score, which in turn will affect the district score. Now the high school is asking the department, "How can we support your improvement efforts?" and the district is asking the high schools, "How can we support your improvement efforts?" because all three levels are addressing the same indicator, and all three are dependent on the quality of multiple team decisions about instruction and curriculum for their respective scores to improve.

An example of the district indicators aligned to a math department team's results is shown in figure 5.3 (page 102). This example is based on summative data and shows the team's math achievement results expressed through common district indicators. The virtue of this team dashboard is that it quickly links team results to district targets. However, this example would not be helpful to the team in diagnosing daily instructional adjustments to address the gaps on the dashboard. For that purpose, the team's formative results are much more appropriate.

The operational response in this example depends on school and team results. In schools where school and team targets have been met or exceeded and those targets match or exceed the district target, math teams can focus on enriching instruction and on those relative few who failed to meet the target. For schools and teams that met their school targets but fell short of the district target, there is more improvement work ahead. In schools and teams that failed to meet their own targets, it is past time for teams to seriously address alternative intervention strategies to boost math achievement overall. In each instance, aligning school and team indicators with the same district indicator drives new improvement efforts, though specific efforts vary from school to school.

Key: ▨ Reached target   ▨ Improving over baseline but not yet at target   ■ No improvement over baseline

ISEL: Illinois Snapshot of Early Literacy; ISAT: Illinois State Achievement Test; NWEA-MAP: Northwest Evaluation Association–Measures of Academic Progress

Goal	Indicator	Measure	When	Baseline	Target	Current
GOAL ONE: Continuously improved student growth and achievement	Students meeting/exceeding expectations on state assessments compared to benchmark districts	ISEL* K–2 reading/math	Annual	76/70	80/75	78/70
		ISAT* 3–8 reading/math/writing/science	Annual	78/72/65/74	80/75/70/80	81/74/64/78
	Students meeting/exceeding college readiness standards compared to benchmark districts	ACT 11 reading/math	Annual	74/76	78/80	75/80
		College readiness assessments: English/math	Annual	65/71	70/75	66/70
	Students meeting/exceeding district grade-level/course learning expectations	K–5 grade-level district learning expectations: reading/math	Trimester	72/72	80/80	75/78
		6–8 grade-level district learning expectations: reading/math/science/social science/writing	Trimester	68/65/71/64/65	75/75/75/70/70	70/71/75/68/65
		Course district learning expectations: reading/math/science/social science	Semester	57/64/66/61	65/70/70/70	60/68/66/70
	Students reading at grade level	K–5 DRA grade-level reading score expectation fall/spring	Fall and spring	65/72	70/75	68/72
		3–8 NWEA-MAP reading/math growth scores fall/spring	Fall and spring	68/74	75/80	70/78
		3–12 IEP goals	Annual	88	90	87
	Students meeting/exceeding personal goals/ growth targets	NWEA-MAP reading/math growth scores fall/spring	Fall and spring	66/75; 68/74	70/80; 72/80	70/78; 71/78
		3–8 IEP goals	Annual	78	80	78

Goal	Indicator	Measure	When	Baseline	Target	Current
GOAL ONE: Continuously improved student growth and achievement *(continued)*	Students receiving passing grades during report card periods	5–8 end of course/level grades: A/B/C	Annual	17/33/29	20/35/30	18/35/30
	Students receiving passing grades during report card periods	9–12 end of course grades: A/B/C	Semester	14/26/35	18/30/40	15/35/38
	Course failures	Course grades: failing English/math/science/social science	Semester	15/19/16/14	12/15/12/10	15/18/14/14
	Increasing number of students in advanced placement courses at middle and high school/ students who received a 3 or higher on AP exams	Students in middle and high school honors/high school advanced placement courses/high school students who receive a 3 or higher on AP (advanced placement) tests	Semester or annual	288/95	300/100	285/96
	Decreasing performance gaps between subgroup populations	Subgroups not meeting AYP	Annual	3: SES, ELL, Sp Ed	1 Sp. Ed	2: Sp Ed, SES
	Students make successful transition to post high school education/career	Student alum satisfaction survey percent agree/strongly agree	Annual	78	85	80

Figure 5.1: District scorecard example for achievement.

ISAT examples used are Illinois State Achievement Tests

Key: ▨ Reached target   ▨ Improving over baseline but not yet at target   ■ No improvement over baseline

Goal	Indicator	Measure	When	Baseline	Target	Current
GOAL ONE: Continuously improved student growth and achievement	Students meeting/exceeding expectations on state assessments compared to benchmark districts	ACT 11 reading/math	Annual	72/74	78/80	78/70
	Students meeting/exceeding college readiness standards compared to benchmark districts	College readiness assessments: English/math	Annual	69/72	70/75	66/70
	Students meeting/exceeding district grade-level/course learning expectations	District course learning expectations: reading/math/science/social science	Semester	55/63/67/66	65/70/70/70	64/64/66/70
	Students reading at grade level	9–12 IEP goals	Fall and spring	33	40	38
	Students receiving passing grades during report card periods	9–12 end of course grades: A/B/C	Semester	16/24/28	20/28/32	18/35/30
	Course failures	Course grades: failing English/math/science/social science	Semester	15/19/16/14	12/15/12/12	15/18/14/14
	Increasing number of students in AP courses at middle and high school/students who received a 3 or higher on AP exams	Students in high school honors/high school AP courses/high school students who receive a 3 or higher on AP tests	Semester	212/86	225/95	225/96
	Decreasing performance gaps between subgroup populations	Subgroups not meeting AYP	Annual	3: SES, ELL, Sp Ed	1 Sp. Ed	2: Sp Ed, SES
	Students make successful transition to post–high school education/career	Student/alum satisfaction survey: percent agree/strongly agree	Annual	75	80	80

Figure 5.2: High school scorecard example for achievement.

Key: ▢ Reached target ▢ Improving over baseline but not yet at target ■ No improvement over baseline

Goal	Indicator	Measure	When	Baseline	Target	Current
GOAL ONE: Continuously improved student growth and achievement	Students meeting/exceeding expectations on state assessments compared to benchmark districts	ACT 11 math	Annual	74	80	78
	Students meeting/exceeding college readiness standards compared to benchmark districts	College readiness assessments: math	Annual	72	75	70
	Students meeting/exceeding district grade-level/course learning expectations	District course learning expectations: math	Semester	63	70	64
	Students reading at grade level	9–12 IEP goals	Fall and spring	33	40	35
	Students receiving passing grades during report card periods	9–12 end of course grades: A/B/C	Semester	16/24/28	20/28/32	18/35/30
	Course failures	Course grades: failing math	Semester	19	15	18
	Increasing number of students in advanced placement courses at middle and high school/students who received a 3 or higher on AP exams	Students in math high school honors and high school math advanced placement courses/high school math students who receive a 3 or higher on AP tests	Semester	99/40	110/50	92/41
	Decreasing performance gaps between subgroup populations	Subgroups not meeting AYP	Annual	3: SES, ELL, Sp Ed	1 Sp. Ed	2: Sp Ed, SES

Figure 5.3: Math department high school dashboard example for achievement.

Data Management, Collection, and Analysis

The second non-negotiable for a results orientation is data management, collection, and analysis. This reflects the reality that teachers cannot themselves create and maintain a data system that will deliver what they require quickly and in the proper formats. Teachers have limited time even without having to manage data. Yet it is evident that they must frequently access data in order to have an accurate understanding of how their students are learning.

This means that the district, particularly at strategic and tactical levels, needs to support teachers through the development and maintenance of a data system that will provide the data teachers need within the timeframes they most need them. Collaborative teams must commit to actively engaging with such data, and the data system that serves teachers must also be aligned to the data needs of the other levels of the district, so that multiple data systems aren't required.

Table 5.2 illustrates the specific aligned responsibilities each role assumes in ensuring data management, collection, and analysis.

Table 5.2: Role Responsibilities for Data Management, Collection, and Analysis

Strategic	Tactical	Operational
3. Ensure a data management system that provides effective and efficient collection, formatting, timely distribution, review/analysis, and reporting of essential indicators of success over time.	3.1 Produce a data management system that is accurate, easily accessible, and timely for users.	3.1.1 Know how to use the data management system to access data and information in a timely way to make improved learning decisions. 3.1.2 Understand the purposes for all assessment data. 3.1.3 Provide feedback on how to make the data management system more effective and efficient.
	3.2 Produce a data management system that allows for easy input/collection.	3.2.1 Provide input, following data collection policies and procedures, to ensure efficiency. 3.2.2 Use consistent tools and strategies to make data input and collection effective and efficient.
	3.3 Produce a data management system that displays data in a user-friendly format.	3.3.1 Provide input to ensure data is reported in a format that is easy to analyze and act on. 3.3.2 Use consistent tools and strategies to make data analysis effective and efficient.

continued →

Strategic	Tactical	Operational
3. Ensure a data management system that provides effective and efficient collection, formatting, timely distribution, review/analysis, and reporting of essential indicators of success over time. *(continued)*	3.4 Produce a data management system that provides a way to track individual student and cohort student group data over time.	3.4.1 Access student data to regularly report performance results over time to students and parents. 3.4.2 Access student cohort data to regularly report performance results over time to teams and the school.
4. Ensure improvement goals are aligned to the greatest areas of need (GAN).	4.1 Require teams and the school to review all indicators to determine the areas of greatest need.	4.1.1 Identify what is working well and celebrate success. 4.1.2 Identify the greatest areas of need to guide the development of improvement plans.
	4.2 Require schools and teams to interdependently set improvement goals that are specific, measurable, attainable, results oriented, and time bound.	4.2.1 Operationally define the area needing more improvement to develop a shared understanding of what needs improvement. 4.2.2 Collect current baseline data with which the improvement goal can be measured. 4.2.3 Analyze the baseline data and information about best practices and research to assist in identifying possible causes.

Strategic Responsibilities

Strategists set parameters for what are valid, reliable, and timely data-reporting criteria and schedules for all levels of the school system. They do this by identifying standards for data reporting—such as requiring schedules for collection, analysis, and reporting of district scorecard data—and providing the format of the district performance scorecard itself. This format should be echoed in school performance scorecards and grade-level or department dashboards. Agreed-upon criteria for the reporting of student performance results (by grade or department, school, ethnic or SES group, gender, and so on) allow aligned data to flow to the district performance scorecard from all tactical and operational levels of the district.

Strategists reinforce the importance of the agreed-upon criteria by ensuring that the quality of the reporting is as valid, reliable, and timely for the tactical and operational roles as it is for their own. This means a commitment to resources—such as technological support dedicated to data collection and display formatting—that strategists might not otherwise provide. With the alignment of the roles around common indicators, strategists become more appreciative of the tactical and operational challenges around data management and thus become more willing to dedicate resources to that end.

Strategists must make their resource decisions based on an assessment of priorities. Which are the priorities that most deserve the scarce resources available for distribution? And how can a strategist tell? In this instance, priorities can be defined through the identification of greatest areas of need (GAN) (Conzemius & O'Neill, 2001). GAN is a data analysis process that allows a district, school, or team to determine the greatest area of need for any subject area or between subject areas. An example would be looking at student achievement results in the writing areas of organization, conventions, voice, composition, and word choice over a three-year period. By examining the results, the highest-priority area for improvement is the area with the least achievement success.

GANs are not developed by strategists; development is a tactical responsibility. But once identified, GANs can become a strategically effective priority filter. GANs become the drivers for the distribution of resources by identifying PLC areas where data, not a strategist's personal interests or political agendas, say the school or district needs to improve.

Tactical Responsibilities

At a tactical level, administrators need to make sure that data meet standards for validity and reliability and arrive in formats that are easy to understand and access. The standards for data should echo the criteria for SMART goals (page 16). Not only do these criteria establish strong standards for the quality of data, but they also standardize how people will identify and collect their data. This makes the alignment of data across roles more seamless and informative.

Data formats and displays that are helpful to some can be confusing to others. This is a particular concern for teachers; if the data aren't helpful for what they are looking to address or aren't easy to understand or quickly access, teachers will typically abandon them for other tasks. The effective tactician understands these operational data needs and addresses them effectively.

One way to effectively encourage a teacher's use of data is to apply the three basic rules of data: data should be (1) easily accessible, (2) purposefully arranged, and (3) publicly discussed (Many, 2009). But before the three rules can be applied, the issue of preparation time for data must be addressed. Teachers are unlikely to find the time to use any data systematically without tactical support, usually performed by or coordinated through the principal.

An example of the need for such tactical support refers back to the discussion in chapter 2 (pp. 21–22) around the purposes for team performance dashboards. Paperwork required of teams by tacticians and strategists, such as team dashboard formatting and maintenance, should be kept to a minimum, because a team's time together is limited, and that time needs to be spent on improving results from a focus on learning.

Therefore, successfully managing team dashboards starts with a valuation around the time teams should spend in data maintenance. Given a teacher's limited time, *it is far more important for teams to analyze and act on data than it is to spend time formatting those data*. While we embrace the benefits of having teacher teams analyze their results in relation to school and district results, we emphatically contend that the ongoing task of preparing these data should not fall on the shoulders of teams. Data preparation and formatting, unless it can only be done by teachers, represents one more task that is not central to the purpose of the team.

And we certainly do not advocate a team being responsible for crafting multiple data-based displays. If a team's data display meets the needs of the team and those data are aligned to the data required by the school and district, multiple data displays serve no additional purpose even as they demand more time and effort to produce. At this point, form has overcome function, and there is more emphasis on producing data than there is value in the data produced. As in most things, form and function should balance, and a single format that meets the needs of the team and aligns to the needs of the school is recommended.

Even here, tacticians need to carefully protect team time so teams can maximize the amount of time spent analyzing and using data while simultaneously minimizing the time spent collecting and preparing it. This means formatting data for team use becomes a new tactical responsibility. The idea is to create a team-friendly dashboard format and feed the desired data into it so teams can analyze those data rather than format them. The "team-friendly" format requirement addresses data rule #2: data should be purposefully arranged.

So who should do this work? It is a tactical function, but not necessarily a principal's responsibility. It could be the responsibility of a team leader, a department head, a paid extra duty assignment, a team coach, a curriculum specialist, or someone from the tech department. The point is, it can't be an additional load on teams that are expected to both teach and meet regularly to assess the impacts of teaching and learning.

This shouldn't confuse what a team should analyze with what it has time to produce. The proper distinction is not that a team should only gives credence to data it prepares itself; rather, increased strategic and tactical support can make more and better data available to teams. What can seem to be data "busywork" in preparation can become data "treasure" through analysis. Let tacticians assume as much of the data busywork as possible so teams can reap rewards from the data treasure.

Teachers also need data that meets their instructional and planning schedules; they should not have to conform their instruction and planning to the delivery schedule of data. This addresses data rule #1: data should be easily accessible to teams. Collaborative team schedules should drive data delivery. In a similar fashion, team analysis needs should drive the formatting of data. Often, this formatting can be standardized across teams using the same or similarly measured indicators.

Two additional tactical responsibilities include (1) ensuring that team data discussions regularly take place and (2) protecting the privacy of team discussions. These tactical responsibilities address data rule #3: data should be publicly discussed. Principals need to require summaries of team meetings or documented evidence of a team's data analysis conversations in order to monitor whether these discussions are regularly occurring. However, principals also need to ensure that the content of those discussions stays between the team and the principal—such discussions are not shared with the public. Reporting of data, which should be public when it involves scorecard performance data, is far less so when it involves a team's student performance data. Such data should remain private, so those analyzing the largely formative data are not judged too soon or too harshly. Scorecard data are much more summatively driven, and this carries with it a more public reporting obligation.

Operational Responsibilities

Regularly using data creates at least three challenges for teachers at the operational level: (1) the data must be openly shared with the appropriate audiences; (2) the data must be trustworthy enough to identify the greatest area of need for a team, school, or district; and (3) the baseline data must improve teachers' understanding of student growth.

Data Must Be Openly Shared

In discussing the power of collaboration, Sergiovanni (2005) described teams as either congenial, collegial, or collaborative communities of practice, adding that, of these, the collaborative communities of practice are most important. The open sharing of data among teaching colleagues is an important step toward building collaborative communities of practice. Working in isolation, as we have pointed out, deprives the lone teacher of the expertise and experience of his or her colleagues. Openly sharing data promotes a powerful cultural shift from the traditional perspective of *my students in my classroom* to one of collective responsibility for *our students in our school.*

We have also learned that once teachers trust that data will be used to drive instructional decisions rather than to judge an individual teacher's effectiveness, they begin to share, discuss, and value the importance of data. Our experiences support an observation by Lachat and Smith (2005) that any school culture that regularly uses data cannot afford to fear those data if it is expected to embrace them.

Data Must Be Trustworthy

The second operational challenge is trusting the data to drive a team's or school's GAN. Teachers struggle when unexpected data results collide with their own beliefs about teaching and learning. Data results are considered *research-based,* while the blend of a teacher's anecdotal, testimonial, and experiential knowledge is considered *evidence-based.* However, both can be valid. For example, it is ludicrous to suggest that a parent try to quantify how much she loves her child, or that we give a numerical value to describe how much we appreciate a piece of music. Not everything that is knowable is measurable. Some things are just known directly, and resolving any dissonance between what teachers believe based on past experience and what teachers understand based on what the data reveal is a healthy exercise for teams.

The blending of evidence-based and research-based knowledge creates the most powerful context for instructional decision making and continuous improvement in our schools.

Baseline Data Must Improve Understanding

The third operational challenge is in understanding the power of baseline data. For those teachers not accustomed to using them, baseline data—usually derived from a formative assessment—can be viewed as a needless and extra testing burden. After all, experienced teachers have years of evidence-based knowledge at their disposal that has intuitively steered them on an accurate instructional course though many classes of students. Why change now? Where is the value-added benefit that justifies the additional time and effort it takes to manage, collect, and analyze all of these data?

However, for those committed to using data, baseline data become essential; those data are the foundation for determining how much *change* in learning has occurred. A teacher's reluctance to collect baseline data is likely a cue that the notions of measurement and research-based knowledge have yet to break through that teacher's dependence on using only his or her own evidence-based knowledge.

Data-Based Action to Improve Results

The third non-negotiable for a results orientation is data-based action to improve results—that is, what one does as a result of having the benefit of data. This action orientation is encapsulated in Blanchard, Carlos, and Randolph's (2001) observation that "people without accurate information cannot act responsibly; people with accurate information feel compelled to act responsibly" (p. 32).

This application phase, following the analysis of results, represents the heavy lifting required of a commitment to a results orientation.

Table 5.3 illustrates the aligned role-specific responsibilities for data-based action to improve results.

Strategic Responsibilities

This non-negotiable holds strategists accountable for two important responsibilities. The first is to ensure that districtwide improvement plans are aligned to measurable goals and targets. Strategists need to continually say, "It is all well and good that we want to improve, but how will we measure what our improvement should look like?"

If something is important enough to do, it is important enough to measure. However, this doesn't mean strategists create the plan's measurement tools. Tacticians create them. Strategists then approve the plans and measure and monitor their effectiveness.

Table 5.3: Role Responsibilities for Data-Based Action to Improve Results

Strategic	Tactical	Operational
5. Ensure improvement plans are aligned to improvement goals.	5.1 Provide systemwide tools and training to ensure development of improvement plans aligned to improvement goals.	5.1.1 Use the district's systematic process for developing an improvement plan aligned to improvement goals.
		5.1.2 Clarify and assign individual and collective responsibilities for the development of improvement plans aligned to improvement goals.
	5.2 Require schools and teams to work together interdependently to conduct action research that is results oriented.	5.2.1 Develop improvement theories or strategies, and conduct action research in order to improve results.
		5.2.2 Focus on results rather than activities by clarifying how the achievement of goals will be monitored and measured through indicators, measures, and targets.
6. Regularly and publicly review results of the improvement plans to monitor improvement efforts and report progress.	6.1 Monitor improvement theories and strategies to ensure results are improving.	6.1.1 Compare the results of improvement theories and strategies with baseline data to determine if results are improving.
		6.1.2 If results are improving, standardize new theories and strategies into daily practice.
		6.1.3 If results show little or no improvement, investigate alternate theories and strategies.

The second strategic responsibility is to regularly and publicly review the progress made (or not made) toward achieving the improvement plan's targets. The district performance scorecard gives strategists a tool by which to publicly perform this ongoing monitoring responsibility.

The trick is in the ongoing and public monitoring of new data that links to the improvement plans, rather than reporting only when the school or district has addressed or failed to address the plans. The former takes a formative approach to public reporting—it is more beneficial when the public and the staff can see the progress being made toward a strategic improvement target. In a summative view, there is merely a report of success or failure after the fact.

Tactical Responsibilities

Tactical responsibilities center on ensuring that action research in classrooms and the theories and strategies being implemented are actually resulting in measurable improvement. Because the research, theories, and strategies are being played out in real classrooms with real children, the adults in the school system cannot simply experiment for the sake of experimentation alone.

Tacticians therefore have both front- and back-end monitoring responsibilities. At the front end, they require evidence that the action research, theories, and strategies being tried are based on the best available information about best practices. The likelihood of success needs to be high from the outset.

At the back end, tacticians require evidence in the form of artifacts or results that the interventions are making a positive difference. If learning doesn't improve, their continuation cannot be justified, but if evidence shows improvement, the intervention needs to become a priority.

Operational Responsibilities

The responsibilities for operationalists are similarly results-oriented. Teachers need to craft improvement plans that are linked to measurable goals, determine how they will measure the outcomes from their interventions, and collect baseline data by which to compare intervention results.

This is why teachers in a PLC focus on results rather than activities in assessing the effectiveness of their instruction. Though evidence-based information can sometimes be useful in supplying context and more objective results-based information can be determinative, it is the combination of the two that holds the most promise for success.

Alignment Constants

Here the same four alignment constants we applied to the first two big ideas—(1) policies, practices, and procedures; (2) an aligned appraisal system; (3) resources and training; and (4) monitoring and reporting of data—are now applied to a results orientation (see table 5.4).

Strategic Responsibilities

One sure way to achieve the alignment of a district's policies, practices, and procedures is to see if they align to the district's strategic goals. Strategists charge tacticians with carrying out this analysis. Tacticians then assess the results and make recommendations to strategists. This activity is a precursor to aligning the budget to strategic goals, an application of the resources and training constant.

Table 5.4: Alignment Constants for Establishing a Results Orientation

Alignment Constant	Strategic	Tactical	Operational
Policies, practices, and, procedures	7. Require an analysis, by school and district office, of the policies, practices, and procedures that do and do not align with a results orientation, followed by an action plan for addressing those policies, practices, and procedures that are not aligned.	7.1 Produce a summary, by school and district office, of practices and procedures that do not align with a results orientation, and create specific recommendations as to what can be done to better align to that end.	7.1.1 Review policies, practices, and procedures that align with a results orientation. 7.1.2 Celebrate those policies, practices, and procedures that are in alignment, and act on what needs to be changed for those not in alignment.
		7.2 Provide examples of best practices, through literature and experiences, for stakeholders to communicate compelling rationales for making shifts from where we are to where we need to be around a results orientation.	7.2.1 Ensure that teaching practices are in line with best practice research aligned to a results orientation. 7.2.2 Examine present practices and procedures by experimenting with doing things differently to get better results.
Aligned appraisal systems	8. Require that district appraisal systems align the non-negotiables for a results orientation with the standards for performance.	8.1 Ensure that the non-negotiables for a results orientation are aligned to the performance appraisal feedback systems.	8.1.1 Collect appraisal assessment data, aligned to the non-negotiables for a results orientation, through self-, peer/team, and supervisor assessment data. 8.1.2 Use appraisal assessment data to establish professional growth plans and actions that lead to improved student and teacher performance.
		8.2 Use non-negotiables for a results orientation to guide recruitment, selection, induction, retention, mentoring, and professional growth.	8.2.1 Provide input into the recruitment and selection of new staff against the non-negotiables for a results orientation. 8.2.2 Mentor others to develop the capacity to deploy and sustain the non-negotiables for a results orientation.

continued →

Alignment Constant	Strategic	Tactical	Operational
Resources and training	9. Align resources for support and training to ensure systematic and systemic deployment of the non-negotiables for a results orientation.	9.1 Provide opportunities to learn, apply, and reflect on best practices aligned to the non-negotiables for a results orientation.	9.1.1 Participate in professional development to reflect on practice and gain additional tools, skills, strategies, and knowledge to meet district expectations for results-orientation non-negotiables. 9.1.2 Assist colleagues in meeting district expectations for results-orientation non-negotiables.
Monitoring and reporting	10. Require at each level of the system—student, classroom, team/department, school, program, and district—that improvement efforts, through deployment of non-negotiables for a results orientation, be monitored and reported.	10.1 Monitor system requirements through agenda planning and focused discussion to assess progress related to results-orientation non-negotiables. 10.2 Report system requirements through scheduled communication processes to stakeholders.	10.1.1 Examine teaching and learning results to see if improvements are being made based on results-orientation non-negotiables. 10.1.2 Share strategies to further guide improvement or redirect improvement efforts. 10.1.3 Track progress through data charts, graphs, or logs. 10.2.1 Share results through clear communication processes and reporting tools. 10.2.2 Reflect both formatively and summatively on results to be certain improvement efforts are adding value.

Another application of the alignment constants is to require each level—from grade level or department teams to the board of education—to regularly report on improvement efforts using data. This means standardized reporting instruments at each level need to be designed and aligned to each other. Aligned performance scorecards and dashboards (pages 20–23) are ideally suited to address this strategic expectation.

Aligned data reporting means results from one level can be directly connected to data from other levels. Even as targets differ, they can be related through common indicators contained in all dashboards and scorecards.

Tactical Responsibilities

At a tactical level, administrators should develop and use an aligned appraisal system by applying the big idea non-negotiables as a common basis for teacher and administrator performance expectations. Because the appraisal system is aligned across all role levels, it ensures a high level of commitment to the big ideas, no matter who the person or what the position being appraised. This is not to diminish the skills required by specific teaching or administrative positions. Those criteria should also be a part of an aligned appraisal system. But they should not be the only criteria. If the three big ideas are to be the center of a district's vision and values, then people in the district should be appraised according to their performance in "living" the district's vision and values and connecting their work to everyone else's work.

This commitment is no trifling matter. A truly aligned appraisal system represents a massive districtwide commitment and affects recruitment, selection, induction, retention, mentoring, and professional growth expectations for every district teacher and administrator. But it also establishes clear and consistent performance expectations similar to those expected of students. Once an aligned appraisal system is in place, the criteria for success are clear to all and equally applied, just as they are for students in the classroom.

As one of many possible aligned appraisal system examples, this is particularly true for hiring and mentoring. By grounding the selection and training of new staff in the big idea non-negotiables, performance expectations become standard for everyone from the beginning of employment. A results orientation can more quickly become a districtwide reality when people start out already committed to it.

Another aligned appraisal example requires a tactical responsibility that couples with applying the resources and training constant—providing evidence-based and research-based examples of best practices. This is a way to communicate compelling rationales for making shifts from where the school or district presently is to where it needs to be.

To illustrate, the combination of these two constants is demonstrated through a particularly vexing example: What should the districtwide expectations of teachers and administrators be for aligned grading practices and grading criteria? What best practices should drive this discussion? What should teachers be reasonably expected to produce in terms of grading and of what quality? How much of the grading process should be standardized at team, school, or district levels as opposed to being set individually by teacher-based discretion? When should grading practices align to or deviate from the district's non-negotiables?

None of these questions have easy or even definitive answers. But neither can the act of grading be completely divorced from common appraisal expectations simply because it is hard to answer alignment-based questions around grading. And should not an aligned appraisal system make at least make a passing reference to how grading is carried out?

Aligned grading has two foci: (1) what is graded and (2) how grades are determined. In many districts, deep conversations about how to select and align such criteria never occur.

What is graded needs to be agreed upon by all, so grades, from class to class, represent the same attainment of knowledge. This is where grades need to align to the targeted expectations of the guaranteed and viable curriculum. But necessary considerations do not stop there. Exactly how should they align? Does a grade represent attainment of a learning target? Based on summative assessments only? Weighted summative and formative assessments? Class participation? Homework completion? Some combination of all of the above? If so, in what proportions?

Determining grades is about setting common grading criteria. Are grades computed on a percentage or averages basis? What constitutes the difference between an A and a B? A passing versus a failing grade? Should plusses and minuses be used? Are percentage grade cutoffs standard within and across subject areas? In many districts, individual teachers still determine, in isolation, how to compute a grade, and there is normally little standardization among them.

This lack of standardization makes comparisons of grades suspect as a dependable data source. Yet schools spend an inordinate amount of time and energy producing grades. Why shouldn't this time and energy represent results that are valid for a results orientation, given the effort put forth in their development?

Determining common grading systems and grading criteria is still one of the most difficult arguments for a tactician to make and a teacher to hear, in no small part because experts in the field do not always agree on the specifics of how to do so. Indeed, such authorities as Chappuis, Stiggins, Arter, and Chappuis (2005), Marzano (2010), O'Connor (2002), and Reeves (2010b) have all weighed in on various sides of the issue, establishing new interpretations of grading best practices.

It is not our purpose to resolve the debate regarding best practices in grading. Our purpose is to stress that, however they are determined, grading practices need to be common districtwide. What is graded, what constitutes a grade, and the characteristics of common grading criteria must align throughout the district so the results produced can assist in creating the kind of data-enriched environment discussed here.

Unfortunately, common grading actions and criteria rank among the least aligned of current educational practices. So generating this discussion becomes a tactical obligation if alignment is the goal. And given the strong and differing opinions on grading held by so many educators, best practices must drive such discussions if there is to be any hope of arriving at a well-accepted decision.

Operational Responsibilities

The monitoring and reporting constant drives two operational responsibilities related to a results orientation. The first involves the use of artifacts, the second the use of team dashboards. Both supply information teams use to alter future instruction—the "action" part of the non-negotiable data-based action to improve results.

Use of Artifacts

Artifacts represent tangible evidence of a results orientation in two areas of operational responsibility: (1) ensuring that all students learn and (2) ensuring that the department or grade-level teacher team members become learners themselves. Artifacts, along with direct evidence of student learning through products like student tests, writing samples, and so on supply the data found in a team dashboard.

Student achievement artifacts provide evidence of meeting specific and measurable team or department targets aligned to dashboard indicators. How those team and department targets are set should be the product of continual team data study and analysis.

The main requirement should be that targets meet Conzemius and O'Neill's (2002) definition of "compelling yet attainable" (p. 5). That definition, paired with the strategic standard of required annual improvement, guarantees that a target will exceed the previous year's attainment. Improvement is therefore an expected outcome. Only the degree of improvement is in question, and that should be set by department or grade-level teams, with some focused prodding and guidance from the school's principal or school leadership team.

Use of Dashboards

The targets developed by teachers will be reflected in their department or grade-level performance dashboards, generated from their team's learning results analysis and discussions. The targets from the combined department or grade-level dashboards translate to comparable targets for the school performance scorecard. In turn, school scorecard targets translate to comparable targets for the district performance scorecard. In this way, targets at all levels are aligned, because they are driven by classroom-based realities, generated from the bottom up rather than the top down.

With artifacts and targets in place, the context for a team's data analysis is established. Operationally, teams now meet regularly to analyze data; assess successful or unsuccessful instructional plans; engage in rich, evidence-based, and research-informed discussions regarding instructional alternatives; and make the resulting instructional changes in classrooms with students. This last step brings the process back to center: the actions teachers take as a result of their data analysis result in instructional changes that should lead to future improvement in learning.

A final dashboard statement bears repeating: team dashboards need to be easy for teachers to access and utilize. As stated earlier, this means their development and ongoing maintenance should become a tactical responsibility so as little team time as possible is spent in the preparation of data. This makes the area of data support for teams a whole new tactical function, as opposed to simply adding another operational responsibility to teams. In a district fully aligned as a PLC, team time is focused on improving student learning.

Case Study for Establishing a Results Orientation

The following Nirvana School District story illustrates how an attempt to implement a districtwide assessment system failed to serve its purpose of clarifying what a district's students were learning, yet consumed precious principal and teacher time in the process. A lack of alignment in conceptualizing and carrying out this initiative doomed it to controversy.

An Assessment System for All

After attending a summer institute, Assistant Superintendent Ben Korbett made the decision to promote the use of common assessments during the upcoming school year. The board of education's goal-setting process consisted of a brainstorming session to generate a long laundry list of loosely connected pet projects and state-mandated tasks. Adding one more initiative to the list, he reasoned, would not be difficult.

Ben was very proud of the assessment system he had developed. Ten years earlier, he had been promoted directly from the assistant principal's office on the strength of his ability to disaggregate data from annual, high-stakes, nationally norm-referenced tests.

With the recent emphasis on state exams, Ben's role had taken on even more prominence, and his intricate data-based board presentations had become legendary. Each year, the board report became more complex, more colorful, and—in Ben's own words—"more compelling." After all, every year brought another year of longitudinal data showing that the level of student achievement remained remarkably—well—average, but at least it was stable.

Districtwide data retreats, first initiated by Superintendent Sue Stanfield and board president Fran Ackers, had been in place for a few years, and teachers had gotten comfortable with looking over the data Ben identified as being most important. Principals no longer objected to writing school improvement plans based on data that were months old, and once he presented the school improvement plans to the board, they were carefully filed in his office.

The data retreats were definitely an "A-list event," but the newly designed semester exams were Ben's pride and joy. He took the improvement targets generated by the data retreats and carefully selected items for the semester exams from an item bank he had purchased the previous year. Ben retained sole access to the items; after all, teachers did not have the time or expertise to write tests that would generate valid and reliable results. That was his job.

Teachers association president Barbara King had frequently complained that items on the semester exams did not match classroom instruction, but Ben had held his ground. Even if the items did not match what was being taught, they certainly matched what was being tested by the state. Despite Barbara's frequent criticisms, no one other than the occasional isolated teacher complained that there was no connection between the state assessment and classroom instruction. Ben did not feel compelled to simply buckle to another union gripe, of which there were already far too many!

The best thing about the semester exams was they were safe, secure, and efficient. The exams themselves were a closely guarded secret. Copies were not released until the Monday of testing week. Each principal was required to sign for his or her exams and return the exact same number to Ben's office by Friday.

His secretary, Ruth Moss, carefully and meticulously checked individual teachers' names off a list, and any recalcitrant teachers were bombarded with a relentless stream of caustic emails until they complied with the test security procedures. Ben was certain that teachers were grateful that he had stepped up and was willing to coordinate logistics for the semester exams. It was a lot of work!

Once the semester exams were scored and Ben had analyzed the results, a memorandum comparing everyone's results was sent to the principals, who, in turn, copied the memorandum and distributed everyone's data to the entire team—all at the same time, of course. There were no surprises.

Ben was convinced everyone appreciated having someone of his statistical ability and background prepare a report summarizing the results. That spring, he was in the midst of preparing a new report for the board using data from the most recent annual state assessment. The new report would show that student achievement remained unchanged and the high school had failed to make AYP (adequate yearly progress, a state-defined minimum school achievement level) for the second consecutive year.

Contrary to what Ben believed, however, it had long since become painfully obvious to school staff that there was no support for the semester exams initiative. Principals, department chairs, and classroom teachers had been left out of the planning process and therefore had little investment in either the assessment system or its results. When the results finally did arrive, they were typically relegated to a shelf to gather dust.

Privately, the teachers association, led by Barbara King, criticized the board for allowing Ben to "bully teachers" and dictate instructional priorities. Principals complained they had no input into the details of how semester exams were administered and did not see the results until well into March. They continually heard teachers argue the exams were a waste of valuable instructional time. In fact, the next spring, the teachers association began the bargaining process with a demand to limit the amount of testing to no more than 10 percent of instructional time.

The board was caught off guard and couldn't remember why the idea of promoting common assessments had been added to the list of annual goals. When challenged by Fran Ackers, Sue Stanfield could not articulate why the district was testing the students so often or what the goal was designed to achieve.

The entire situation was frustrating and embarrassing, and questions about the assessment system were growing. With nodded agreement from other board members, Fran demanded at a public board meeting that the principals explain how this disaster could have been allowed to happen. But the principals, highly embarrassed, had no answers since they and all of their staff had been left out of the development of plans for implementing the mandate.

When Ben learned of the board's displeasure, he was dumbfounded. How could anyone object to a system that was clearly so accurate and well designed? He could not begin to fathom how things could have suddenly gone so wrong.

Deconstructing the Story: What Went Right

Actually, a lot of things were done right, even though this entire project ended up poorly.

Strategic

- Promoting the use of common assessments across the district was central to both a focus on learning and a results orientation.

- A results orientation required that teachers become accustomed to seeing and analyzing data on student achievement. Of course, the data received should have been relevant to what the teachers were teaching.

- School improvement plans were rightly presented to—and approved by—boards of education.

- Generating improvement targets at the data retreat was potentially a highly desirable collaborative effort for a results orientation. That effort could have been successful if it had been grounded in a variety of different data on student achievement, if the principals and teachers had credible input into in what targets should be, if targets had been allowed to vary team by team and school by school, and if the indicators for the targets had been sufficiently standardized for districtwide reporting.

- There is nothing wrong with an accurate and well-designed assessment system. But more than just accurate and well designed, an assessment system's results have to be relevant and helpful to those who are directly trying to improve student learning.

Tactical

- Certainly the ability to accurately disaggregate data from nationally norm-referenced, high-stakes tests was appropriate if those tests were aligned to essential learning targets that were district priorities for all students. The issue is not how well the data were disaggregated but to what learning targets these data were aligned.

- Establishing districtwide data retreats is an excellent practice that can get everyone on the same data page if the data are not only shared but analyzed and interpreted together by all role levels.

- Semester exams—a means by which to determine if day-to-day teaching is meeting learning targets—are a highly desirable indicator for a results orientation, assuming those exams are tied tightly to learning targets that reflect what is regularly taught in classrooms.

- Questions on the semester exams should certainly match what is being tested by the state. But those questions should also match the learning targets every teacher is teaching in classrooms.

- There is nothing wrong, in and of itself, with tracking the release and distribution of high-stakes testing materials. It depends on how that tracking is done, and especially whether school staff, who provide the tests to students, are considered allies or impediments to the process.

Operational

- Having the assistant superintendent score the test results did relieve an unnecessary burden from the school staff. Of course, the real issue is not that it is the assistant superintendent who scores the tests, but that the scoring is competently done by someone who can relieve the schools of this load.

Deconstructing the Story: What Went Wrong

Yet, given all of the things done right, this particular story had a very bad ending. What went wrong? And why did what went wrong trump all of the things that appeared to be sound independent actions or decisions?

Strategic

- There was no strategic leadership by which to define and hold to common expectations for the district. The assessment system the assistant superintendent developed was not attached to a larger purpose beyond its own creation. It became an end in itself rather than a means to an end. Making it "legendary" didn't make it relevant, especially to the teachers who were doing the heavy lifting in the classroom every day.

- The assistant superintendent confused his monitoring role in assuring the usefulness of the assessments with making the system entirely his own in order to guarantee his own importance. By cutting key tactical and operational players (principals and teachers) out of the development and management of the system, he killed any incentive for those in the schools to discern any relevance from its use.

- The assistant superintendent, for all of his data skills and training, went well beyond his monitoring role by micromanaging the management of this data at school levels, thus killing school-based support for the assessment system.

- Only selective principles of a professional learning community were applied. A focus on summative assessments results alone, without an accompanying focus on collaboration and a more expanded notion of what comprises valid results (formative as well as summative), doomed this particular effort. The three big ideas of a professional learning community don't effectively change things piecemeal; they must be aligned in their applications.

- The assistant superintendent should never have been allowed to simply add his own pet project to the school system's list of strategic goals.

- The board and superintendent were caught off guard, but they shouldn't have been. Had clear, strategic, and aligned expectations been set from the beginning, the semester exams would never have been allowed to take on a life of their own.

Tactical

- There needed to be more behind a results orientation than simply the results from one annual high-stakes assessment.

- The "compelling" nature of the annual report was apparently more based on the fireworks in the presentation than to any alignment to what was happening instructionally in classrooms. A truly compelling report should be tied directly to what the learning targets are, what was done to successfully meet them, and what needs to be done differently for targets not met.

- Stable test score results over the years means continuous improvement is *not* occurring, regardless of the level—high or low—of the scores themselves.

- The assistant superintendent should certainly have contributed his notions as to what the important take-aways from the data results were, but it was not his job alone to do so. More important, what were the take-aways from the schools—from the principals and teachers who were directly responsible for improving student achievement?

- Data that are months old have very limited usefulness. At the very least, the assistant superintendent should have been linking this summative data in his board report to more frequent formative data that could show levels of ongoing progress and improvement.

- While purchasing items was not in and of itself an issue, a lack of alignment between what was being taught versus what was being tested was an issue.

- The assistant superintendent's refusal to relinquish the reins on test questions let a golden collaborative opportunity slip by that might have developed more teacher and principal support for the semester exams.

- The assistant superintendent was ignoring operational feedback from the association president and isolated teachers that was crucial to establishing an effective results orientation. In this case, some relevant operational expertise was ignored because of the source of the information—the teachers association.

- Tight security for the exams was not a bad thing in and of itself. But this level of security should have been an obvious signal to the assistant superintendent that his exam didn't have the support of the school staff.

- The caustic emails were certainly not going to help engender the collaborative effort and commitment required to support these exams.

- This story confused *a lot of work* with the *work's value*. These exams are indeed a lot of work for the assistant superintendent, but in this case, the value was minimal since they were not supported at the school level.

- It appeared that the assistant superintendent was the sole interpreter of the results. No wonder teachers and principals resented the exam! And once again, an opportunity to gain collaborative involvement and commitment was lost.

- The assistant superintendent's ability and background in testing metrics was being used as an excuse to assume that school staff wanted and appreciated what he was doing.

- The state student achievement results were not good: student achievement overall was unchanged, and the high school failed AYP for the second consecutive year. Exactly how were the assistant superintendent's semester exams helping improve learning results?

- No wonder the principals couldn't explain the semester exams to the board, as they had no say in their development or implementation. But having to publicly refute their assistant superintendent at the board meeting to defend themselves would put them in an embarrassing trap with no way out.

Operational

- The 10 percent bargaining demand by the teachers association was a perfect example of a bad proposal designed to address a legitimate problem. The association's proposal assumed all assessments were as troublesome as the semester exams, which was not the case.

- Because no one else in the school system intervened to solve the semester exam issues, the association stepped in. So the issue escalated to a power struggle among roles over the wrong solution to a legitimate problem.

Here is what this story could have looked like had the district been fully aligned toward a results orientation.

Revisiting the Story

At a strategic level, the board held its annual data retreat with the board, Superintendent Sue Stanfield, Assistant Superintendent Ben Korbett, all of the Nirvana principals and assistant principals, the data department staff, the teachers association president Barbara King, each school's association representative, and the team leaders from every school all in one room to discuss, together, the implications of results from a number of sources, both formative and summative. The teachers and principals were the lead speakers, with more tactical and strategic perspectives added later. The results of this data dialogue were consensus-driven, tied to predetermined district goals, and linked by portfolio artifacts through performance scorecard and dashboard results, which had already identified the indicators with which to guide the data discussion.

The data retreat was functionally designed to use the results to monitor the school district's strategic goals, reflected through the various indicators. The data discussions held few surprises for anyone, because all had previously noted ongoing progress from scorecards and dashboards throughout the previous school year. The data dialogue wasn't about discovering anything new; rather, it was about assessing what had happened during the past school year and why, and setting the groundwork for new targets. Those targets would emerge from the district performance scorecard and schools' targets, with the only tight requirement being that targets for the coming year needed to exceed attainments from the previous year or, for multiyear targets, to reflect measurable gains from the previous year's results.

The board and superintendent did not set random goals representing pet projects. Their goals aligned directly to a strategic mission, vision, and values and to districtwide goals that succinctly described what the district considered its most pressing strategic priorities. Sue and the board did not allow their goals to be supplemented by tacticians or operationalists. Instead, they previously had been open to considerable tactical and operational, as well as community, input in initially developing the goals.

The board and Sue had already set the standards for the alignment of classroom instruction to curricula to learning targets to state standards; the proper blend of formative and summative assessments; common templates for reporting artifacts at tactical and operational levels; the use of SMART goal data for goal setting and reporting; the requirements of district, school, and department and grade-level performance dashboards; and the establishment of improvement targets reflected in the scorecards and dashboards. Strategically, growth measures were converted to district targets for student achievement improvement. And the board's fiscal monitoring, aided by projections from board finance chairman George Bell and his committee, ensured that resources needed to implement a focus on results would have been prioritized in the budget, including resources for the necessary staff development and training needed for implementation.

At a tactical level, Assistant Superintendent Ben Korbett had already established the assessment system's standards and general parameters with the help of the Nirvana principals and an ad hoc committee of teacher team leaders. Ben focused his efforts at monitoring rather than ownership and control, because he understood his job was not to produce the assessment system. Rather, it was to ensure an assessment system was produced that was the result of collaborative tactical and operational efforts and met the new strategic standards.

His particular expertise in assessment metrics was valuable, but no more so than the school-based tactical expertise of principals and the operational expertise of teachers. Ben realized with each of those areas of expertise combined, the resulting assessment system had a far better chance of being useful to all and therefore embraced by all.

The emphasis for the development of the assessment system was not on the flash of the presentation but rather on its overriding purpose—the aligning of data that would both inform daily instruction and monitor progress toward performance scorecard and dashboard indicator targets.

Finally, the connection between the results of the assessment system and those reporting on it was clear from the start. Ben was not the sole reporter to the board. He made sure principal and teacher input and analysis were heavily represented, and he shared the reporting responsibilities with them. Ben became much more like the conductor of a symphony rather than a one-man band.

Thus, the board was not confused in terms of going to the principals to figure out what went wrong. And under an aligned assessment system, things weren't nearly so likely to go wrong.

The board also didn't need to go to Ben with questions, because he didn't have to answer all of those questions himself—even though he was responsible for the quality and alignment of the assessment system. His guiding coalition of principals and teachers, who were partners in both its creation and implementation and had personal commitments of their own to the assessment system, was there to help him. And there were ample formative and summative results to access for the team to explain any questions that might arise.

One lesson from this story is that when something in the school system is implemented that isn't working, it doesn't pay to "wait it out." If the implementation is grinding the district-level gears, waiting it out—"standing firm" and "holding his ground," as the assistant superintendent did in response to critical operational feedback—doesn't eventually smooth things out. It makes the grinding worse, because a misalignment among the gears (the three role perspectives) is not being addressed.

In this case, complaints to the board and the negotiating stance of the teachers association were not first-time responses. They were last-time responses, born of a mounting frustration. As the gears ground on, the responses and reactions to the continual grinding became more strident, and the task of identifying a satisfactory solution became much more difficult.

Summary

The solution is not to turn the whole process over to the schools and just let them figure it out. That plan is bereft from the other direction—now central office and strategic expertise are needed in order to craft the right result. The expertise of *all* of the roles is required—strategic guidance from the board and superintendent, tactical expertise and standardization expectations from central office administrators, tactical expertise in terms of school culture and resource needs from principals, and operational expertise from teachers regarding what is really happening with student learning in classrooms.

When all roles are aligned, successful implementations and sustained improvement are the result. If role alignment around a collaborative culture is a valid approach, then should not role alignment applied to a results orientation be a valid approach as well?

Professional learning communities represent an integrated approach to changing the cultures and products of schools. Role alignment represents the means by which to make the promise of PLCs come alive. The combined result is a fully aligned district— in this case, fully aligned toward a successful results orientation.

Conclusion

This chapter discussed the importance of aligning both the reporting of results and the actions taken as a response to them. We examined the three non-negotiables of a results orientation—(1) a data mindset; (2) data management, collection, and analysis; and (3) data-based action—and looked at the role responsibilities for each of them. We presented the connection between valid, reliable, and timely results and having those results convert to new information to drive change at every level. Then we deconstructed a story to illustrate the consequences of a lack of alignment in conceptualizing and carrying out an initiative to establish districtwide common assessments, before retelling the story with a more successful and aligned approach driving events.

The final chapter looks at two instruments that a district can use to self-assess its alignment capacities. These alignment appraisal instruments can help a district determine its alignment strengths and its opportunities for improvement.

chapter six

An Alternative to Dead Reckoning: Assessing PLC Alignment

What's the use of running if you are not on the right road?

—German proverb

To align a district as a professional learning community requires data that can provide accurate feedback as to whether or not a district's alignment efforts are on course. But a long journey will only become longer when, instead of a reliable compass, dead reckoning—essentially navigating by guesswork—is used as the guide. Because objective data are required to accurately assess the strengths and improvement opportunities for districtwide alignment efforts, moving in the right direction requires district-level appraisal tools to serve as that compass.

This chapter will discuss two such appraisal tools; by using them, districtwide alignment efforts don't have to rely on dead reckoning for progress assessment. The first tool measures alignment across the three big idea non-negotiables, while the second focuses on implementing the alignment constants.

Why Alignment Appraisal Tools?

Quint Studer (2003) observes that:

> measuring the important things helps organizations define specific targets, measure progress against those targets, and align the necessary resources to achieve them. Measurement supports the alignment of desired behaviors. It excites the organization when goals are achieved. Measurement holds individuals accountable for the results and helps to determine if things are working.

Measurement aligns specific leadership and employee behaviors that cascade throughout the organization to drive results.(p. 61)

Studer's medically based observation can be applied equally to school districts. People in a school district need assessment tools to tell them how they are doing, and the district itself needs assessment tools to objectively describe its progress and results.

These tools need to measure both results *and* processes. Schmoker (1999) makes this point when he states, "Concentrating on results does not negate the importance of process. On the contrary, the two are interdependent. . . . Processes exist for results and results should inform processes" (p. 4).

The most important data for districts, just as for schools and teams, answer the question "How well are our students learning?" But districts also need implementation data that declare whether certain districtwide implementations around the non-negotiables—targeted resource ability and deployment, climate for learning, climate for teaching, and customer satisfaction—are occurring as desired.

The Big Idea Assessment Instrument— Appraisal Tool 1

This self-evaluation tool assesses the impacts of each of the non-negotiables. It is designed to directly assess the operational responsibilities of a typical PLC team of teachers. Tacticians and strategists assess themselves to the degree that they enable and support the districtwide application of this tool's operational responsibilities.

Table 6.1 (pages 127–129) is an example of how this tool works, showing a collaborative team's hypothetical ratings for a self-assessment for the focus on learning non-negotiables. (A blank form for each of the big idea assessment instruments can be found in the appendix and online at **go.solution-tree.com/plcbooks**.)

In the table, there are two ratings for a guaranteed and viable curriculum and three ratings each for a balanced and coherent system of assessment and a schoolwide pyramid of interventions. These eight ratings, based on the three focus on learning non-negotiables, suggest this district has prioritized its initial focus on learning efforts in aligning a common curriculum to achievement standards and expectations and that those efforts are now regularly demonstrated by a majority of the district's teachers. A majority of teachers also now use formative assessments to guide their instructional decisions (row E, column 4).

However, the systematic reporting of learning results is not as far along, even though districtwide efforts have begun in this direction (column 3). For example, it can be surmised from the results that there is not yet alignment among common formative and summative assessments across the district, given the solitary 4 rating for the use of formative assessments.

Table 6.1: Big Idea Assessment Instrument for the Focus on Learning Non-Negotiables

Focus on learning: We acknowledge that the fundamental purpose of our school is to help all students achieve high levels of learning. We are therefore willing to examine all of our practices in light of their impact on learning.

Non-negotiable: A guaranteed and viable curriculum	1 Haven't begun to address this issue (0)	2 Talking but no action yet (0)	3 Have begun to address this issue (1)	4 Have moved beyond implementation (2)	5 Process deeply embedded in our culture (3)
A We work with colleagues on our team to build shared knowledge regarding state standards, the district curriculum guide, and their trends regarding student achievement and expectations for the next course or grade. This collective inquiry has enabled each member of our team to clarify what all students must know and be able to do as a result of every unit of instruction.				X	
B We use those targets to design our unit and lesson plans and to communicate priority expectations to students and their families. We report progress related to those essential learning targets formatively and summatively. We focus time at conferences to identify essential targets where mastery has been achieved and essential targets where continuous learning is necessary. We assist students in taking responsibility to track their mastery of those essential learning targets.			X		

continued →

Non-negotiable: A balanced and coherent system of assessment	1 Haven't begun to address this issue (0)	2 Talking but no action yet (0)	3 Have begun to address this issue (1)	4 Have moved beyond implementation (2)	5 Process deeply embedded in our culture (3)
C We have a balance between common formative assessment data to guide instruction and learning and common summative assessment data to reflect on the success of our teaching.			X		
D We monitor the learning of each student on all essential learning targets on a timely basis through a series of frequent, team-developed formative assessments that are aligned to learning standards and measurable benchmarks. Our assessment system includes common unit preassessments, midpoint feedback, end-of-unit assessments, trimesterly or end-of-grading-period assessments, and end-of-year assessments. We share ideas for providing daily/weekly feedback.			X		
E We use the data from formative assessments to guide instructional differentiation decisions, pacing decisions, and intervention decisions.				X	

Non-negotiable: A schoolwide pyramid of interventions	1 Haven't begun to address this issue (0)	2 Talking but no action yet (0)	3 Have begun to address this issue (1)	4 Have moved beyond implementation (2)	5 Process deeply embedded in our culture (3)
F	We provide a system of interventions that guarantees each student will receive additional time and support for learning if he or she experiences initial difficulty.			X		
G	We require rather than invite students to devote the extra time and receive the additional support until they are successful.		X			
H	We have developed strategies to extend and enrich the learning of students who have mastered essential learning targets.		X			

Adapted from DuFour, DuFour, Eaker, & Many (2006), Learning by Doing. Used with permission.

There is more work to do with a guaranteed and viable curriculum and a balanced and coherent system of assessments to get ratings of at least four in the five non-negotiable areas represented. This situation makes districtwide implementation efforts around a schoolwide pyramid of interventions a secondary priority. Interventions are "on this district's radar," but because of cascading effect concerns, they are not yet being emphasized for implementation.

The numbers in parentheses below the column headings ("We have not begun to address this issue") rate the overall level of implementation. Because the first two columns both indicate the same issue—that implementing the specific non-negotiable area has not yet begun—both columns are given a 0 value. The remaining three columns range from 1 for initial implementation to 3 for deeply embedded implementation. The three implementation levels, along with the five column ratings, allow the big idea appraisal instruments to be scored on either three- or five-point scales.

The strategic and tactical efforts to support the teams' implementation efforts are measured by the alignment constants instrument, the focus of the next section.

The Alignment Constants Instrument— Appraisal Tool 2

The alignment constants instrument (figure 6.1) provides an alignment constants–based appraisal tool for assessing a school or district's PLC progress.

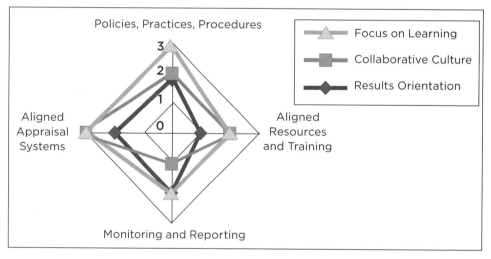

Figure 6.1: Alignment constants instrument.

The alignment constants instrument measures the implementation of each big idea expressed through its alignment constants. If each of the four constants is successfully deployed for each of the three big ideas, they will, in combination, be able to drive the culture and performance of the district.

Figure 6.1 represents a radar diagram in which 0 represents no application and 3 represents a fully aligned application. Nancy R. Tague (2005) states that "a radar diagram is a graphical method of displaying multivariate data in the form of a two-dimensional diagram of three of more quantitative variables represented on axes starting from the same point" (p. 437). A radar diagram is used to highlight strengths and weaknesses.

The alignment constants instrument allows for twelve different measurement points: four alignment constants for each of the three big ideas. The ideal rating—representing a fully aligned application of each alignment constant for each big idea—would be twelve 3s.

In the hypothetical example in figure 6.1, a focus on learning is making progress in policies, practices, and procedures; monitoring and reporting; and resources and training (all 2s). However, it is still weak in aligned appraisal systems (1). A collaborative culture is strong in aligning its resources and training (3), is progressing with policies, practices, and procedures and aligned appraisal systems (both 2s), but is weak in monitoring and reporting (1). A results orientation is strong in policies, practices, and procedures and resources and training (both 3s) and is making progress in monitoring and reporting and aligned appraisal systems (both 2s).

Based on this alignment constants instrument example, the weakest areas—and therefore the next areas of districtwide concentration—are aligned appraisal systems for a focus on learning and monitoring and reporting for a collaborative culture (both 1s).

The overriding purpose of the alignment constants instrument is to align the entire district along expectations around the non-negotiables through measures around the four alignment constants. As a result, the district—not just isolated schools or classrooms within the district—progresses along the PLC journey in measurably identifiable ways.

Conclusion

The two appraisal tools just discussed provide ample data by which a district can objectively self-assess where it is and where it wants to go in implementing PLC non-negotiables at all levels.

A word of caution: these tools should be used as *formative* rather than summative appraisal instruments. Successful implementation of the big ideas of a PLC, particularly districtwide, is an ongoing journey, not a one-time event. These tools are designed to help districts assess their progress along that continual journey and to address the most pressing districtwide non-negotiables without overloading the district's capacity to address them. Note, however, that no matter what the results from these tools, if student achievement goals are not being met, the district is still not improving; the results of these two appraisal instruments cannot stand alone.

These tools are not designed to summatively rate a school system as successful or unsuccessful in aligning to the big ideas of a PLC. They are certainly not designed to summatively evaluate individuals in the school system who carry out the work.

They *are* designed to provide data that will help a district *align* its implementation efforts toward the big ideas of a PLC. Alignment across all district levels is the key to the successful districtwide implementation of a PLC.

> Be really whole and all things will come to you.
>
> —Lao-Tsu

Professional learning communities have shown clear and demonstrated success. Now the challenge is to replicate that success on a larger scale in many districts and across multiple schools. An aligned districtwide approach can deliver on the promise of that success through the delineation of role-based responsibilities that tie directly to the three big ideas of a PLC.

While this is anything but a simple approach, it is far from an impossible one. *Aligning School Districts as PLCs* lays out a framework for what each district role does best—aligned to the work of the other roles—in order to move an entire district to commit to the three big ideas. It is the combination of individual role expertise and the alignment of the expert work of all three roles—both coupled to the muscle of the three big ideas—that make such an approach successful.

Individual and professional autonomy (loose), on the one hand, and districtwide standardization and mutual accountability (tight), on the other, are the two conflicting forces that must align for real districtwide change to take hold. This is the balance Reeves (2005) was referring to when he wrote that "the leaders of professional learning communities balance the desire for professional autonomy with the fundamental principles and values that drive collaboration and mutual accountability" (pp. 47–48).

Professional learning communities have proven adept at balancing autonomy and standardization through an elegant blending of non-negotiables and individual creativity around the three big ideas. Therefore, this goal should be within sight of every district. One needs only a sound and accurate navigational tool to guide one's journey.

Aligning School Districts as PLCs seeks to provide that navigational tool. Although it may never be fully completed, the journey itself provides its own rewards, rewards that compound with the distance traveled.

We believe aligning the work of a district across all levels is the organizational equivalent of ensuring that every student learns. We also believe that aligning the work of schools and districts around the big ideas of a professional learning community gives integrity to both the district and to every employee's work.

At the beginning of this book, we asked that you join us on this alignment journey. At the end, we ask that you continue that journey with increased commitment, even as you come ever nearer to your destination.

Big Idea Self-Assessments

Schools can use the blank forms in this section to measure their level of implementation of the three big ideas of a professional learning community. There is one self-assessment for each of the three big ideas.

Self-Assessment for a Focus on Learning

Focus on Learning: We acknowledge that the fundamental purpose of our school is to help all students achieve high levels of learning, and therefore we are willing to examine all of our practices in light of their impact on learning.

Non-negotiable: A guaranteed and viable curriculum	1 Haven't begun to address this issue (0)	2 Talking but no action yet (0)	3 Have begun to address this issue (1)	4 Have moved beyond implementation (2)	5 Process deeply embedded in our culture (3)
A We work with colleagues on our team to build shared knowledge regarding state standards, the district curriculum guide, and their trends regarding student achievement and expectations for the next course or grade. This collective inquiry has enabled each member of our team to clarify what all students must know and be able to do as a result of every unit of instruction.					
B We use those targets to design our unit and lesson plans and to communicate priority expectations to students and their families. We report progress related to those essential learning targets formatively and summatively. We focus time at conferences to identify essential learning targets where mastery has been achieved and essential targets where continuous learning is necessary. We assist students in taking responsibility to track their mastery of those essential learning targets.					

Aligning School Districts as PLCs © 2011 Solution Tree Press • solution-tree.com
Visit **go.solution-tree.com/PLCbooks** to download this page.

Non-negotiable: A balanced and coherent system of assessment	1 Haven't begun to address this issue (0)	2 Talking but no action yet (0)	3 Have begun to address this issue (1)	4 Have moved beyond implementation (2)	5 Process deeply embedded in our culture (3)
C We have a balance between common formative assessment data to guide instruction and learning and common summative assessment data to reflect on the success of our teaching.					
D We monitor the learning of each student on all essential learning targets, on a timely basis, through a series of frequent, team-developed formative assessments that are aligned to learning standards and measurable benchmarks. Our assessment system includes common unit preassessment, midpoint feedback, end-of-unit assessment, trimesterly or end-of-grading-period assessment, and end-of-year assessment. We share ideas for providing daily/weekly feedback.					
E We use the data from formative assessments to guide instructional differentiation decisions, pacing decisions, and intervention decisions.					

Aligning School Districts as PLCs © 2011 Solution Tree Press • solution-tree.com
Visit **go.solution-tree.com/PLCbooks** to download this page.

Non-negotiable: A schoolwide pyramid of interventions		1 Haven't begun to address this issue (0)	2 Talking but no action yet (0)	3 Have begun to address this issue (1)	4 Have moved beyond implementation (2)	5 Process deeply embedded in our culture (3)
F	We provide a system of interventions that guarantees each student will receive additional time and support for learning if he or she experiences initial difficulty.					
G	We require rather than invite students to devote the extra time and receive the additional support until they are successful.					
H	We have developed strategies to extend and enrich the learning of students who have mastered essential learning targets.					

Adapted from DuFour, DuFour, Eaker, & Many (2006), Learning by Doing. *Used with permission.*

Self-Assessment for Building a Collaborative Culture

Focus on Collaboration: We are committed to working together to achieve our collective purpose of learning for all students. We cultivate a collaborative culture through the development and support of high-performing teams.

Non-negotiable: Shared mission, vision, values, and goals	1 Haven't begun to address this issue (0)	2 Talking but no action yet (0)	3 Have begun to address this issue (1)	4 Have moved beyond implementation (2)	5 Process deeply embedded in our culture (3)
A	We have developed and deployed mission, vision, values (collective commitments), and goals to set clear direction for our district, our school, and our team/department.					
B	We recognize that specific behaviors and actions embody the vision, mission, values, and goals in our daily work. We identify the collective commitments we make to one another to ensure attainment of our mission, vision, values, and goals.					
C	We promote, through those specific behaviors and actions, a culture/teaching environment of personal growth and high performance. We foster shared accountability for continuous improvement.					

page 1 of 3

Non-negotiable: High-performing collaborative teams	1 Haven't begun to address this issue (0)	2 Talking but no action yet (0)	3 Have begun to address this issue (1)	4 Have moved beyond implementation (2)	5 Process deeply embedded in our culture (3)
D We are organized into high-performing, collaborative teams in which members work together interdependently to achieve common goals. We have developed and adhere to team norms and protocols.					
E We are provided time during the contractual day and school year to meet as a team. We support both vertical and horizontal team collaboration. We address transition and articulation from elementary to middle to high school and beyond.					
F We create a safe environment to report and compare data so as to learn from one another and share best practices.					
G We follow protocols that define how collaborative team time is to be used and artifacts that document how collaborative team time has been used.					

Aligning School Districts as PLCs © 2011 Solution Tree Press • solution-tree.com
Visit **go.solution-tree.com/PLCbooks** to download this page.

Non-negotiable: Intentional collaboration	1 Haven't begun to address this issue (0)	2 Talking but no action yet (0)	3 Have begun to address this issue (1)	4 Have moved beyond implementation (2)	5 Process deeply embedded in our culture (3)
H We use team time to engage in collective inquiry on questions specifically linked to gains in student achievement.					
I Each team is called upon to generate and submit products, which result from its work on the critical questions related to student learning. We know how the decisions we make during collaboration affect learning results.					
J We recognize and celebrate individual and team success aligned to our goals.					

Adapted from DuFour, DuFour, Eaker, & Many (2006), Learning by Doing. Used with permission.

Self-Assessment for a Results Orientation

Focus on Results: We assess our effectiveness on the basis of results rather than intentions. Individuals, teams, and schools seek relevant data and information and use that information to promote continuous improvement.

Non-negotiable: Data mindset: Efficacy and transparency	1 Haven't begun to address this issue (0)	2 Talking but no action yet (0)	3 Have begun to address this issue (1)	4 Have moved beyond implementation (2)	5 Process deeply embedded in our culture (3)
A	We establish a safe, data-enriched district, school, and team/department culture where we can share and compare results data as a way to demonstrate accountability and learn from one another.				
B	We commit to aligning our work to the long-range goals and indicators/measures by which the district and school define our success.				
C	We set district, school, and team/department goals that are specific, measurable, attainable, results-oriented, and timely. They address our gaps in relationship to the long-range district and school indicators/measures.				
D	We set indicators, measures, and challenging yet attainable targets for our goals to be clear about what is most important to track and monitor for improvement.				
E	We emphasize and promote outcomes over inputs and results over activities.				

Non-negotiable: Data management, collection, and analysis	1 Haven't begun to address this issue (0)	2 Talking but no action yet (0)	3 Have begun to address this issue (1)	4 Have moved beyond implementation (2)	5 Process deeply embedded in our culture (3)
F	We design and use a data management system that is valid and reliable, easily accessible, and provides timely and user-friendly feedback.					
G	We collect and analyze data and information to be certain we are addressing the needs and requirements of our stakeholders.					
H	We analyze data to: (a) identify students who need additional time and support for learning, (b) discover strengths and weaknesses in our individual teaching, (c) help measure our team's progress toward its goals, and (d) define our action plans.					
I	We ensure that students take responsibility for their own learning by collecting data to monitor and track their performance compared to high expectations and performance results of others.					

Aligning School Districts as PLCs © 2011 Solution Tree Press • solution-tree.com
Visit **go.solution-tree.com/PLCbooks** to download this page.

Non-negotiable: Responsibility for action to improve results	1 Haven't begun to address this issue (0)	2 Talking but no action yet (0)	3 Have begun to address this issue (1)	4 Have moved beyond implementation (2)	5 Process deeply embedded in our culture (3)
J	We share responsibility to act on data and develop plans to change present practices when our results are not where we want them to be.					
K	We develop and test improvement theories/strategies based on our analysis and current results to be certain they are adding value and improving results.					
L	We share evidence to show our results are improving compared to the past.					
M	When results have not improved, we develop and test new theories and strategies while eliminating those that did not change results.					

Adapted from DuFour, DuFour, Eaker, & Many (2006), Learning by Doing. Used with permission.

Barth, R. (2006). Improving relationships within the schoolhouse. *Educational Leadership*, 63(6), 8–13.

Beatty, C. A., & Scott, B. A. B. (2004). *Building smart teams: Roadmap to high performance*. Thousand Oaks, CA: SAGE.

Blanchard, K., Carlos, J., & Randolph, A. (2001). *Empowerment takes more than a minute* (2nd ed.). San Francisco: Berrett-Koehler.

Bossidy, L., Charan, R., & Burck, C. (2002). *Execution: The discipline of getting things done*. New York: Random House.

Buffum, A., Mattos, M., & Weber, C. (2009). *Pyramid response to intervention: RTI, professional learning communities, and how to respond when kids don't learn*. Bloomington, IN: Solution Tree Press.

Chappuis, S., Stiggins, R., Arter, J., & Chappuis, J. (2005). *Assessment FOR learning: An action guide for school leaders*. Portland, OR: Assessment Training Institute.

Conzemius, A., & O'Neill, J. (2001). *Building shared responsibility for student learning*. Alexandria, VA: Association for Supervision and Curriculum Development.

Conzemius, A., & O'Neill, J. (2002). *The handbook for SMART school teams*. Bloomington, IN: Solution Tree Press.

DuFour, R. (2003). Building a professional learning community. *School Administrator*, 60(5), 13–18.

DuFour, R., DuFour, R., & Eaker, R. (2008). *Revisiting professional learning communities at work: New insight for improving schools*. Bloomington, IN: Solution Tree Press.

DuFour, R., DuFour, R., Eaker, R., & Karhanek, G. (2004). *Whatever it takes: How professional learning communities respond when kids don't learn*. Bloomington, IN: Solution Tree Press.

DuFour, R., DuFour R., Eaker, R., & Many, T. (2006). *Learning by doing: A handbook for professional learning communities at work*. Bloomington, IN: Solution Tree Press.

DuFour, R., DuFour, R., Eaker, R., & Many, T. (2010). *Learning by doing: A handbook for professional learning communities at work* (2nd ed.). Bloomington, IN: Solution Tree Press.

DuFour, R., DuFour, R., & Many, T. (2007). *PLC audit project* [Unpublished workshop handout]. Presented at Schaumburg, IL.

Elmore, R. (2006). *School reform from the inside out: Policy, practice and performance*. Cambridge, MA: Harvard Education Press.

Fuhrman, S., & Elmore, R. (2004). *Redesigning accountability systems for education*. New York: Teachers College Press.

Fullan, M. (2002). The change leader. *Educational Leadership, 59*(8), 16–20.

Fullan, M. (2005a). *Leadership and sustainability: System thinkers in action*. Thousand Oaks, CA: Corwin Press.

Fullan, M. (2005b). Professional learning communities writ large. In R. DuFour, R. Eaker, & R. DuFour (Eds.), *On common ground: The power of professional learning communities* (pp. 209–223). Bloomington, IN: Solution Tree Press.

Fullan, M. (2008). *The six secrets of change: what the best leaders do to help their organizations survive and thrive*. San Francisco: Jossey-Bass.

Fullan, M. (2009, January 27). *The six secrets of change*. Presented at The Six Secrets of Change Midwest Principal's Center Workshop, Naperville, IL.

Fullan, M., Bertani, A., & Quinn, J. (2004). New lessons for districtwide reform. *Educational Leadership, 61*(7), 42–46.

Fullan, M., & Hargreaves, A. (1996). *What's worth fighting for in your school?* (2nd ed.). New York: Teachers College Press.

Guskey, T. R. (2009). Formative assessment: The contribution of Benjamin S. Bloom. In H. Andrade & G. J. Cizek (Eds.), *Handbook of formative assessment* (pp. 106–124). Florence, KY: Routledge.

Hunter, M. (1976). *Improved instruction*. El Segundo, CA: TIP Publications.

IBM. (2003). *The future is open* [Linux television commercial]. Accessed at www.a42.com /node/338 on September 7, 2003.

Kaplan, R. S., & Miyake, D. N. (2010). The balanced scorecard. *School Administrator, 2*(67), 10–15.

Kohm, B., & Nance, B. (2009). Creating collaborative cultures. *Educational Leadership, 67*(2), 67–72.

Kotter, J., & Rothgeber, H. (2006). *Our iceberg is melting: Changing and succeeding under any conditions*. New York: St. Martin's Press.

Lachat, M. A., & Smith, S. (2005). Practices that support data use in urban high schools. *Journal of Education for Students Placed at Risk, 10*(3), 333–349.

Lencioni, P. (2002). *The five dysfunctions of a team: Participant workbook*. San Francisco: Jossey-Bass.

Lewis, C. (2004). Lesson study. In L. B. Eason (Ed.), *Powerful designs for professional learning* (pp. 171–184). Oxford, OH: National Staff Development Council.

Many, T. (2009). Three rules to help manage assessment data. *Texas Elementary Principals and Supervisors Association News, 66*(2), 7, 9.

Marzano, R. J. (2010). *Formative assessment and standards-based grading: The classroom strategies series.* Bloomington, IN: Marzano Research Laboratory.

Marzano, R. J., & Waters, T. (2009). *District leadership that works: Striking the right balance.* Bloomington, IN: Solution Tree Press.

O'Connor, K. (2002). *How to grade for learning: Linking grades to standards.* Thousand Oaks, CA: Corwin Press.

Patterson, K., Grenny, J., Maxfield, D., McMillan, R., & Switzer, A. (2008). *Influencer: The power to change anything.* Columbus, OH: McGraw-Hill.

Peters, T. J., & Waterman, R. H., Jr. (2004). *In search of excellence: Lessons from America's best-run companies.* New York: Warner Books.

Redding, S. (2006). *The mega system: Deciding, learning, connecting—A handbook for continuous improvement within a community of the school.* Lincoln, IL: Academic Development Institute.

Reeves, D. (2005). Putting it all together: Standards, assessment, and accountability in successful professional learning communities. In R. DuFour, R. Eaker, & R. DuFour (Eds.) *On common ground: The power of professional learning communities* (pp. 45–63). Bloomington, IN: Solution Tree Press.

Reeves, D. (2006). *The learning leader: How to focus school improvement for better results.* Alexandria, VA: Association for Supervision and Curriculum Development.

Reeves, D. (2008). *Developing a data mindset.* Englewood, CO: The Leadership and Learning Center.

Reeves, D. (2010a). *Transforming professional development into student results.* Alexandria, VA: Association for Supervision and Curriculum Development.

Reeves, D. (2010b). *Elements of grading.* Bloomington, IN: Solution Tree Press.

Riel, M. (2006). *Learning circles.* Accessed at www.iearn.org/circles/lcguide on April 4, 2011.

Schmoker, M. (1999). *Results: The key to continuous school improvement.* Alexandria, VA: Association for Supervision and Curriculum Development.

Senge, P. (1990). *The fifth discipline: The art and science of the learning organization.* New York: Currency Doubleday.

Sergiovanni, T. (2005). *Strengthening the heartbeat: Leading and learning together in schools.* San Francisco: Jossey-Bass.

Sparks, D. (2005). The final 2%: What it takes to create profound change in leaders. *Journal of the National Staff Development Council, 26*(2), 8–15.

Sparks, D. (2007). *Leading for results: Transforming teaching, learning, and relationships in schools* (2nd ed.). Thousand Oaks, CA: Corwin Press.

Sparks, S. (2008). Creating intentional collaboration. In C. Erkens, C. Jakicic, L. G. Jessie, D. King, S. V. Kramer, T. W. Many, et al., *The collaborative teacher* (pp. 31–55). Bloomington, IN: Solution Tree Press.

Studer, Q. (2003). *Hardwiring for excellence*. Gulf Breeze, FL: Firestarter.

Tague, N. (2005). *The quality toolbox*. Milwaukee, WI: American Society for Quality, Quality Press.

Van Clay, M., & Soldwedel, P. (2009). *The school board fieldbook: Leading with vision*. Bloomington, IN: Solution Tree Press.

Index

The School Board Fieldbook: Leading With Vision
Mark Van Clay and Perry Soldwedel
Take a reader-friendly tour through the responsibilities and challenges of being a school board member. Award-winning administrators give practical guidance on how to best work with school administrators and staff to create and fulfill a shared vision of school system excellence.
BFK269

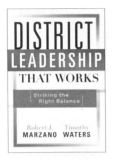

District Leadership That Works: Striking the Right Balance
Robert J. Marzano and Timothy Waters
Bridge the divide between administrative duties and daily classroom impact with a leadership mechanism called "defined autonomy." Learn strategies for creating district-defined goals while giving building-level staff the stylistic freedom to respond quickly and effectively to student failure.
BKF314

Leaders of Learning How District, School, and Classroom Leaders Improve Student Achievement
Richard DuFour and Robert J. Marzano
Together, Dr. DuFour and Dr. Marzano focus on district leadership, principal leadership, and team leadership, and address how individual teachers can be most effective in leading students—by learning with colleagues how to implement the most promising pedagogy in their classrooms.
BKF455

Learning By Doing: A Handbook for Professional Learning Communities at Work™
Richard DuFour, Rebecca DuFour, Robert Eaker, and Thomas Many
The second edition of *Learning By Doing* is an action guide for closing the knowing-doing gap and transforming schools into PLCs. It also includes seven major additions that equip educators with essential tools for confronting challenges.
BKF416

Solution Tree | Press   *a division of*   Solution Tree

Visit solution-tree.com or call 800.733.6786 to order.